Literacy-Building Booklets
Famous Americans

Lucia Kemp Henry

New York • Toronto • London • Auckland • Sydney
Mexico City • New Delhi • Hong Kong • Buenos Aires

Teaching *Resources*

Edited by Immacula A. Rhodes

Cover design by Maria Lilja

Interior design by Sydney Wright

Cover and interior illustrations by Lucia Kemp Henry

ISBN–13: 978-0-545-13369-2
ISBN–10: 0-545-13369-6

Contents

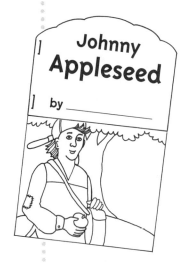

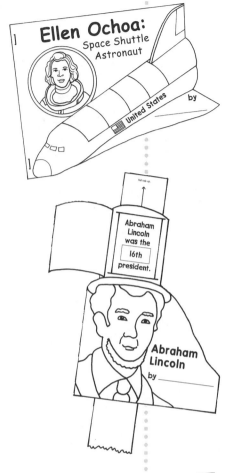

Introduction

Welcome to *Literacy-Building Booklets: Famous Americans*—a delightful collection of unique, interactive booklets for young learners. These 25 booklets help children explore the lives of a diverse group of Americans who have inspired, challenged, and helped shape the people and laws of our nation.

As children learn about these important people, they'll also build comprehension skills and gain valuable reading practice. The interactive booklet formats offer fresh, engaging opportunities to strengthen early literacy skills by exposing children to key concepts of print. By making and "reading" these booklets, children begin to understand that:

* print carries meaning
* words are read from left to right and top to bottom
* letters create particular sounds
* reading should be careful and even-paced

The booklets and activities in this resource facilitate vocabulary development by exploring the lives and accomplishments of important Americans. They also provide children with repeated opportunities to listen, speak, and follow directions, thereby improving their oral language skills. You can use the activities to introduce the featured persons, teach new facts, and reinforce previously learned information, as well as develop vocabulary, explore concepts of print, build background knowledge, boost comprehension, and much more!

Literacy-Building Booklets: Famous Americans is packed with reproducible pattern pages that make preparation of booklets and projects a breeze. For most booklets, simply copy the pattern pages for each child, collect the materials listed, and you're ready to go! As children color, cut, glue, and write to make the booklets, they'll be intrigued by the engaging formats—slide-through, accordion, 3-D, lift-the-flap, and shape books—and will also develop their fine motor skills.

But completing the booklets is only half the fun! After they construct the booklets, invite children to use them to share their knowledge about the fascinating Americans with classmates, family members, and friends. You'll find that proud young readers will insist on reading their booklets again and again, boosting their reading confidence and abilities!

About This Book

What's Inside?

The booklets—organized by the date of birth of the featured Americans—can be easily integrated into your curriculum at any time of the year. For each booklet, you'll find a teaching page that includes the following:

Facts to Share ★★★★★★★★★★★★★★★★★★★★★★★★★★★★★★

You can share these important and interesting facts with children as you introduce and discuss the person. But don't limit yourself to only the information provided in this section. You might research books, the Internet, and other resources to build your own background knowledge and to gather additional information, facts, and pictures to share with children.

Introducing the Activity ★★★★★★★★★★★★★★★★★★★★★★★★

Use the activity in this section to introduce the person to children and set the stage for making the booklet. The activity helps you tap into children's prior knowledge, build background knowledge, and expand vocabulary.

Materials ★★★★★★★★★★★★★★★★★★★★★★★★★★★★★★★★★★

Check this section to find what materials each child will need to complete the booklet. For most, basic art supplies—such as crayons, scissors, and glue—are all you need. The reproducible pattern pages listed for most activities make your preparation time minimal. To make binding the booklets fast and simple, have a few staplers on hand.

What to Do ★★★★★★★★★★★★★★★★★★★★★★★★★★★★★★★★★

This section includes easy, step-by-step directions for making and assembling the booklets. You might want to make each booklet in advance so that you'll be familiar with the steps and have a sample to show children.

Book Break ★★★★★★★★★★★★★★★★★★★★★★★★★★★★★★★★

Suggestions for nonfiction books about the person are provided along with a brief summary of those books. Read or review the books ahead of time to become familiar with their content and illustrations. As you share facts and other information from the books, you might paraphrase or summarize some parts to help children better understand the content.

Taking It Further ★★★★★★★★★★★★★★★★★★★★★★★★★★★★★

The activities in this section compliment and enrich student learning about the person. They provide engaging opportunities to reinforce important concepts, strengthen literacy skills, and broaden learning.

More Facts About . . . ★★★★★★★★★★★★★★★★★★★★★★★★★★

Share the additional facts in this section to give more information and insight about the person's life, experiences, and accomplishments.

Connections to the Standards

This book is designed to support you in meeting the following standards for grades K–1 as outlined by Mid-continent Research for Education and Learning (McREL), an organization that collects and synthesizes national and state standards.

Language Arts

Uses the general skills and strategies of the writing process
- uses drawings to express thoughts, feelings, and ideas
- uses writing and other methods (using letters or phonetically spelled words, telling, dictating) to describe persons, places, objects, or experiences
- writes in a variety of forms or genres (picture books, information pieces, messages, response to literature)

Uses grammatical and mechanical conventions in written compositions
- uses knowledge of letter-sound relationships to write simple words
- uses conventions of spelling in writing (spells level-appropriate high frequency and phonetically regular words)
- uses conventions of print in writing (uses uppercase and lowercase letters, spaces words, writes from left-to-right and top-to-bottom)
- knows that there are rules for forming sentences

Uses the general skills and strategies of the reading process
- uses meaning clues (picture captions, title, cover, story structure, topic) to aid comprehension and make predictions about content
- uses basic elements of phonetic analysis (letter-sound relationships, vowel sounds, blends, word patterns) to decode unknown words
- understands level-appropriate sight words and vocabulary

Uses reading skills and strategies to understand and interpret a variety of informational texts
- uses reading skills and strategies to understand a variety of informational texts (written directions, captions, labels, informational books)

- understands the main idea and supporting details of simple expository information
- summarizes information found in text (retells in own words)
- relates new information to prior knowledge and experience

Uses listening and speaking strategies for different purposes
- uses new vocabulary to describe feelings, thoughts, experiences, and observations
- uses descriptive language
- listens for a variety of purposes
- follows one- and two-step directions
- contributes to group discussions and follows the rules of conversation
- asks and responds to questions
- uses level-appropriate vocabulary in speech

History

Understands how democratic values came to be, and how they have been exemplified by people, events, and symbols
- knows English colonists who became revolutionary leaders and fought for Independence from England (George Washington, John Hancock, Paul Revere)
- understands how individuals have worked to achieve the liberties and equality promised in the principles of American democracy and to improve the lives of people from many groups (Rosa Parks, Cesar Chavez, Martin Luther King, Jr.)
- understands the reasons that Americans celebrate certain national holidays
- knows why important buildings, statues, and monuments are associated with national history

Kendall, J. S., & Marzano, R. J. (2004). *Content knowledge: A compendium of standards and benchmarks for K-12 education.* Aurora, CO: Mid-continent Research for Education and Learning. Online database: http://www.mcrel.org/standards-benchmarks/

George Washington

Children learn about our first president's different careers.

George

Washington

by _____

Facts to Share ★★★★★★★★★★★★★★★★★★★★★★★★★★★★★★★★★★

George Washington had several careers over his lifetime. As a young adult, he farmed the land at his beloved Mount Vernon home as well as the land that belonged to his half-brother. At age 21, he entered the Virginia militia and become a major. He rose to the position of general and led the Revolutionary army. In 1789, he was elected the first President of the United States. George Washington was a successful farmer, military leader, and government official.

Introducing the Activity ★★★★★★★★★★★★★★★★★★★★★★★★★★★

Invite children to tell what they know about George Washington. Then share the facts on this page (above and at right) as a discussion-starter about the different careers of this great man. Afterward, invite children to make these booklets that highlight the careers of George Washington.

What to Do ★★★★★★★★★★★★★★★★★★★★★★★★★★★★★★★★★★

1. Cut out the booklet backing, cover, pages, and word boxes.

2. Color the backing. Write your name on the cover. Then glue the appropriate word box to the cover where indicated.

3. Read pages 1–4. For each page, find the word that completes the sentence. Glue that word box to the page where indicated.

4. Sequence the pages, stack them behind the cover, and staple them to the backing where indicated.

5. Read the booklet together. Then form small groups and have children share their booklets with each other.

Materials

For each child:
★ booklet patterns (pages 32–34)
★ scissors
★ crayons
★ glue

To share:
★ stapler

Taking It Further ★★★★★★★★★★★★★★★★★★★★★★★★★★★★★★★★

Lead a discussion about George Washington's favorite occupation—farming at Mount Vernon. Then invite children to draw a picture of a farm. Have them write or dictate a sentence on their paper about the kind of work George Washington may have done on his farm. Collect the pages and bind them together to create a class book titled "George Washington: Farmer."

More Facts About . . . George Washington
(1732–1799)

• His favorite boyhood subject was Math.

• He started a surveying business at age 17.

• He was over six feet tall.

• He never lived in Washington, D.C.

• He introduced the mule to America!

Book Break ★★★★★★★★★★★★★★★★★★★★★★★★★★★★★★★★★★

Discover George Washington: Farmer, Soldier, President by Patricia A. Pingry (Ideals Children's Books, 2005). This book describes Washington's illustrious careers.

George Washington by Philip Abraham (Children's Press, 2002). Young readers learn about the life of George Washington.

Johnny **Appleseed**

by _____

Materials

For each child:
★ booklet patterns (pages 35–36)
★ scissors
★ crayons

To share:
★ stapler

More Facts About . . . Johnny Appleseed
(1774–1845)

• He often traveled barefoot and wore old clothing.
• He did not own a house.
• He gave to the needy and cared deeply for animals—even insects!
• He could make medicines from plants.
• He ate a vegetarian diet.

Johnny Appleseed
Children learn how a tree grower made life a little sweeter for American settlers!

Facts to Share ★★★★★★★★★★★★★★★★★★★★★★★★★★★★★★

Johnny Appleseed—whose real name was John Chapman—was born in a log cabin on September 26, 1774. He spent his childhood learning about plants and animals in the woods of Massachusetts. At age 18, he moved west and began planting apple trees in the Ohio Valley. Appleseed traveled throughout Connecticut, Massachusetts, New York, Pennsylvania, Ohio, and Indiana. As he went, he planted apple orchards, sold the trees, and taught settlers how to care for them.

Introducing the Activity ★★★★★★★★★★★★★★★★★★★★★★★★★

Ask children to tell where apples come from. Discuss how apples grow and how people care for apple trees. Then use the facts (above and at left) to introduce children to this interesting figure. Finally, invite them to make these booklets about how this unique pioneer helped early settlers in America.

What to Do ★★★★★★★★★★★★★★★★★★★★★★★★★★★★★★★★★★

1. Cut out the booklet backing, cover, and pages.
2. Read the directions at the top of each page, then draw a picture.
3. Color the picture on the backing. Write your name on the cover.
4. Sequence the pages, stack them behind the cover, and staple them to the booklet backing where indicated.
5. Read the booklet together. Then form small groups and have children share their booklets with each other.

Taking It Further ★★★★★★★★★★★★★★★★★★★★★★★★★★★★★★

Cut a poster-sized apple shape from red bulletin board paper. Add a green paper stem and leaf. At the top of the apple write "Johnny Appleseed liked apples because . . ." Then ask children to discuss why they think Appleseed loved apples so much. Write each child's response on the big apple. When finished, display the apple on a wall or bulletin board in the classroom.

Book Break ★★★★★★★★★★★★★★★★★★★★★★★★★★★★★★★★★★★

Johnny Appleseed by Christin Ditchfield (Children's Press, 2003). Simple text and interesting pictures tell the story of John Chapman.

Sacagawea

*Children learn about a Native American woman
who helped early Americans explore the west.*

Sacagawea

by _____

Facts to Share ★★★★★★★★★★★★★★★★★★★★★★★★★★★★★★★★

As a child, Sacagawea—a Shoshone—was captured by a band of Hidatsa
people. A few years later, she married a French man and had a son. In
1805, the Lewis and Clark expedition hired Sacagawea to help them speak
and trade with the Shoshone people as they explored the west. Sacagawea
traveled with the group, along with her husband and son, serving as
translator and guide. She remained with the group on their trip to and from
the Pacific Ocean.

Introducing the Activity ★★★★★★★★★★★★★★★★★★★★★★★★★

Share facts (above and at right) about Sacagawea, then explain that the Lewis
and Clark expedition traveled on horseback, on foot, and by canoe since
there were no roads, cars, or trains at that time. Discuss what it would be
like to travel by these methods and the difficulty the explorers might have
had when crossing high mountains, rowing down raging rivers, and passing
through dense forests. Afterward, have children make these foldout booklets
to highlight the types of landforms encountered by Sacagawea and the
expedition as they traveled.

What to Do ★★★★★★★★★★★★★★★★★★★★★★★★★★★★★★★★★★★

1. Cut out the booklet pages.
2. Glue the pages together where indicated by matching the symbols.
3. Color the cover and the back end of the canoe. Write your name on
   the line.
4. On each page, draw a picture of the named landform.
5. Accordion-fold the booklet so that the cover is on top.
6. Read the booklet together, unfolding it one page at a time to create a
   long canoe. Later, pair up children and have them read their booklets to
   each other.

Taking It Further ★★★★★★★★★★★★★★★★★★★★★★★★★★★★★★

Invite students to examine a large topographical map of the western United
States. Point out the Rocky Mountains in Montana and have children
describe how the mountains look on the map. Then help children trace
the route taken by the Lewis and Clark expedition, counting the mountain
ranges that the explorers probably had to cross on their way to the
Pacific Ocean.

Book Break ★★★★★★★★★★★★★★★★★★★★★★★★★★★★★★★★★★★

Sacajawea by Joyce Milton (Grosset & Dunlap, 2001). Large text,
pronunciation guides, and simple maps in this easy reader help children
learn about Sacajawea and her travels with Lewis and Clark.

Materials

For each child:
★ booklet patterns
  (pages 37–38)
★ scissors
★ glue
★ crayons

★
More Facts About . . .
Sacagawea
(ca. 1787–1812)

• In the Hidatsa language, Sacagawea
  means "bird woman."

• She was born in the part of the country
  that is now known as Idaho.

• She was about 17 years old when she
  joined the explorers.

• She carried her baby in a snug pack on
  her back.

• A mountain pass and a river are named
  for her.

Materials

For each child:
* ★ booklet patterns (pages 39–40)
* ★ scissors
* ★ crayons
* ★ glue

More Facts About . . . Abraham Lincoln
(1809–1865)

* He worked as a storekeeper and a postmaster.
* He was a U.S. Congressman.
* He kept two pet goats, named Nanny and Nanko, at the White House.
* He often held his son, Tad, in his lap while he worked!
* At 6' 4" tall, he holds the record for being the tallest president of the U.S.

Abraham Lincoln

Children learn about a popular president's unusual hat habit!

Facts to Share ★★★★★★★★★★★★★★★★★★★★★★★★★★★★

Often young children connect an image of a tall stovepipe hat to Abraham Lincoln, the 16th president of the United States. This hat style was very popular during Lincoln's time, but he used his for purposes other than making a fashion statement—he stored legal documents, bills, and notes inside his hat! In fact, Lincoln is so well known for this unusual habit that one of his hats is displayed in the Chicago History Museum.

Introducing the Activity ★★★★★★★★★★★★★★★★★★★★★★

Share the facts (above and at left), then help children make a connection to Abraham Lincoln by asking how many of them like to wear hats. Invite them to tell about their favorite hats and to explain why they like them. Then have children make these slide-through booklets so they can share about important ways that Lincoln used his famous hat!

What to Do ★★★★★★★★★★★★★★★★★★★★★★★★★★★★★★

1. Cut out the booklet backing, cover, text strips, and word boxes.
2. Color the backing and cover (hat pattern). Write your name on the line.
3. Cut the two slits at the top of the backing.
4. Glue the cover to the left side of the backing where indicated.
5. Glue the text strips together where indicated by matching the symbols.
6. Read each sentence on the strip. Find the word that best completes the sentence. Then glue that word box to the strip where indicated. Write your own sentence about Lincoln on page 6.
   (Answers: 1. *16th*, 2. *tall*, 3. *hat*, 4. *notes*, 5. *in*)
7. Thread the strip through the slits, as shown.
8. To read the booklet, have children open the hat cover and pull the strip through the slits to reveal one page at a time.

Taking It Further ★★★★★★★★★★★★★★★★★★★★★★★★★★

To make a stovepipe hat, cover an oatmeal canister with black construction paper. Cut a black tagboard circle that's larger than the bottom of the canister and glue it to the bottom to make a hat rim. Add a black crepe-paper band around the lower section of the hat. Then, to reinforce related vocabulary, label index cards with words such as *hat, tall, roomy, black, Lincoln, short, white,* and *small.* Have children read each word and then place that card in the hat if it describes Lincoln's stovepipe hat.

Book Break ★★★★★★★★★★★★★★★★★★★★★★★★★★★★★★

Abraham Lincoln by Wil Mara (Children's Press, 2002). Simple text, photographs, and interesting art tell the story of our 16th President.

Susan B. Anthony

Children learn about how a determined woman fought to win the right to vote for women.

by _____

Many years ago,
American women could not
_____
_____ .

Facts to Share ★★★★★★★★★★★★★★★★★★★★★★★★★★★★★★★★★★★★★

At one time, only men in our country could vote. Susan Brownell Anthony made it her life's work to try to get a law passed that would grant women the right to vote. Because of her hard work and determination, Congress passed the 19th Amendment to the U.S. Constitution in 1920. Women finally had the right to vote! In 1979, the Susan B. Anthony dollar was issued to honor her work for women's rights.

Introducing the Activity ★★★★★★★★★★★★★★★★★★★★★★★★★★★★★

Invite children to tell you what the word *vote* means. Help them understand that when our country was young, voting rights were not granted to all Americans. Share the facts (above and at right), then explain that Susan B. Anthony and many others worked very hard to pass laws that granted all adult Americans the vote. Afterward, have children make these booklets to read to family and friends.

What to Do ★★★★★★★★★★★★★★★★★★★★★★★★★★★★★★★★★★★★★★★

1. Cut out the booklet backing, cover, and pages.

2. Sequence the pages and staple them to the backing where indicated.

3. Color the picture on the backing and write your name on the line.

4. Read the title and circle the word *vote*.

5. Read each page, then write *vote* on the line.

6. Read the booklet together. Then form small groups and have children share their booklets with each other.

Taking It Further ★★★★★★★★★★★★★★★★★★★★★★★★★★★★★★★★★★★

Although children are too young to vote in real elections, give them a taste of the right they will have as adults! Organize a vote about something the entire class participates in, such as a recess activity or book selection for storytime. Present two choices, then have children cast their votes by secret ballot. Invite them to vote on a new "issue" each day for a week to help reinforce how their vote can make a difference!

Book Break ★★★★★★★★★★★★★★★★★★★★★★★★★★★★★★★★★★★★★★★

Susan B. Anthony by Lucile Davis (Capstone Press, 1998). This book is filled with historic photos that illustrate Anthony's life.

Materials

For each child:
★ booklet patterns (pages 41–42)
★ scissors
★ crayons
★ pencil

To share:
★ stapler

★ More Facts About . . . Susan B. Anthony

(1820–1906)

• She could read and write by age 5!

• She was able to get a good education at a time when most women could not.

• As a teacher, she was paid less than male teachers.

• Susan was arrested in 1872 for trying to vote.

• She didn't live long enough to see women get the right to vote—she died in 1906.

• She also worked to get the 15th Amendment passed, which granted African-American men the right to vote.

Harriet
Tubman

] by _____

Materials

For each child:
★ booklet patterns
   (pages 43–45)
★ scissors
★ pencil
★ crayons

To share:
★ stapler

More Facts About . . .
Harriet Tubman
(1820–1913)

• She worked as a house servant and in the fields during her slavery years.

• She followed the North Star at night when she escaped to Pennsylvania.

• She returned to slave country many times to help rescue others from slavery.

• She could not read or write.

• She lived to be over 90 years old.

Harriet Tubman

Children learn about a former slave who helped others find freedom.

Facts to Share ★★★★★★★★★★★★★★★★★★★★★★★★★★★★★★★★

Born a slave in Maryland, Harriet Tubman escaped to Pennsylvania—a state that allowed slaves to live freely—in 1849. Then she began to help her family and other slaves escape to freedom. Working with the Underground Railroad, which was a secret network of people and safe places, she helped more than 300 slaves make the journey to free states. Tubman also worked as a cook, a nurse, and spy during the Civil War.

Introducing the Activity ★★★★★★★★★★★★★★★★★★★★★★★★★★★★★

After sharing facts (above and at left) about Harriet Tubman, explain that the Underground Railroad was not a real railway, but was a secret connection of people and places that worked together to help slaves escape to freedom. Invite children to share their thoughts about how those who were part of the Underground Railroad might have felt whenever they helped someone reach freedom. Then have them create these booklets to share what they know about Harriet Tubman.

What to Do ★★★★★★★★★★★★★★★★★★★★★★★★★★★★★★★★★★★★

1. Cut out the booklet backing, cover, and pages.

2. Write your name on the cover.

3. Color the pictures on pages 1–6.

4. Trace the word on page 7.

5. Sequence the pages, stack them behind the cover, and staple them to the backing where indicated.

6. Read the booklet together. Then form small groups and have children share their booklets with each other.

Taking It Further ★★★★★★★★★★★★★★★★★★★★★★★★★★★★★★★★★

Have children locate Maryland and Pennsylvania on a large map of the United States. Cut a length of yarn that measures the distance between the capitals of these two states. Then explain that during Tubman's time, many slaves traveled from southern to northern states. Ask children to take yarn measurements of the distance between capital cities in various southern and northern states. Help them convert the distances to miles (use the map scale) and then compare their findings to the distance that Harriet traveled to Pennsylvania.

Book Break ★★★★★★★★★★★★★★★★★★★★★★★★★★★★★★★★★★★★

Harriet Tubman by Wil Mara (Children's Press, 2002). This book includes fascinating facts about Harriet Tubman and her courageous life.

Clara Barton

Children learn about a woman who cared for soldiers and others in need.

Facts to Share ★★★★★★★★★★★★★★★★★★★★★★★★★★★★★★★★

Clara Barton lived in Washington D.C. when the Civil War started. She saw that the army was unprepared to take care of wounded soldiers, so she collected and delivered medical supplies to the battlefield. Her nursing services in the field earned her the nickname "Angel of the Battlefield." After the war, she traveled to Europe and learned about a new organization that helped war victims—the Red Cross. When she returned home she established the American Red Cross.

Introducing the Activity ★★★★★★★★★★★★★★★★★★★★★★★★★★

Share the facts (above and at right) about Clara Barton. Then ask children to tell about ways in which they might work with their family or friends to help others in their community who are in need. List their responses on chart paper. Afterward, review the list, inviting children to express how helping others makes them feel. Finally, have them make these booklets to learn more about Clara Barton.

What to Do ★★★★★★★★★★★★★★★★★★★★★★★★★★★★★★★★★★

1. Cut out the booklet backing, cover, and pages.

2. Follow these directions to complete each page:

    page 1: Draw a picture of a letter.

    page 2: Draw a house.

    page 3: Draw a horse pulling a wooden wagon.

    backing and page 4: Color the picture. Then write your name on the line. Draw a red cross on page 4.

3. Sequence the pages, stack them behind the cover, and staple them to the backing where indicated.

4. Read the booklet together. Then form small groups and have children share their booklets with each other.

Taking It Further ★★★★★★★★★★★★★★★★★★★★★★★★★★★★★

Draw a large Red Cross symbol on chart paper. Brainstorm with children some of the ways that the American Red Cross organization helps people in our country today. Add their responses around the symbol to create a poster.

Book Break ★★★★★★★★★★★★★★★★★★★★★★★★★★★★★★★★★★

Clara Barton by Wil Mara (Children's Press, 2002). This book chronicles Miss Barton's long service to our country.

Materials

For each child:
★ booklet patterns (pages 46–47)
★ scissors
★ crayons

To share:
★ stapler

More Facts About . . . Clara Barton
(1821–1912)

• She cared for her injured brother when she was only 11 years old.

• She started the first free public school in New Jersey.

• She held a job working at the U.S. Patent Office earning the same salary as males.

• She led the effort to try to identify missing Civil War soldiers.

• She lived to be 90 years old.

John Muir

*Children learn about a special man who loved
and wanted to protect nature.*

Facts to Share ★★★★★★★★★★★★★★★★★★★★★★★★★★★★★★★★★

After studying nature in college, John Muir walked across the country, sailed
to Cuba and Panama, and then traveled to California. There, he first saw
and fell in love with the Sierra Nevada mountains and Yosemite Valley. Muir
thought it was important to protect the forests and natural areas of that
region. Through his writings and other efforts, he worked to convince the
government to adopt a national conservation program. In 1890, the Sequoia
and Yosemite national parks were established, and Muir became known as
the "Father of the National Park System."

Introducing the Activity ★★★★★★★★★★★★★★★★★★★★★★★★★★★

After sharing facts about John Muir (above and at left), invite children to
tell about their own experiences of visiting natural areas such as local, state,
or national parks. Explain that Muir's efforts to protect and preserve nature
have had some part in making these areas available for people to enjoy.
Afterward, invite children to make these foldout booklets about John Muir.

What to Do ★★★★★★★★★★★★★★★★★★★★★★★★★★★★★★★★★★★★

1. Cut out the booklet patterns.

2. Glue page 2 to page 3 where indicated.

3. Follow these directions to complete each page:

   cover: Write your name on the line.

   page 1: Draw a fish in the river.

   page 2: Draw another animal.

   page 3: Draw another tree.

   pages 4 and 5: Color the picture.

4. Accordion-fold the booklet so that the title page is on top.

5. Read the booklet together, unfolding it one page at a time to create a tall
   picture. Later, pair up children and have them read their booklets to
   each other.

Taking It Further ★★★★★★★★★★★★★★★★★★★★★★★★★★★★★★★★

Invite children to draw a picture of their favorite outdoor place, such as
the woods, a beach, or a city, state, or national park. Have them write (or
dictate) a sentence to tell why it's important to conserve natural outdoor
places. Then bind children's pages together to create a class book titled
"Lessons We Learned From John Muir."

Book Break ★★★★★★★★★★★★★★★★★★★★★★★★★★★★★★★★★★★★

John Muir by Wil Mara (Children's Press, 2002). Young readers learn about
the life and work of this amazing conservationist.

Materials

For each child:

★ booklet patterns
  (pages 48–49)
★ scissors
★ glue
★ crayons

More Facts About . . .
John Muir
(1838–1914)

• He was born in Scotland.

• He wrote books about America's
  natural beauty.

• He loved sleeping outside!

• He said "Let us do something to make
  the mountains glad."

• In 1892, he started the Sierra Club, an
  organization dedicated to conserving
  and protecting wildlands.

Alexander Graham Bell

*Children discover how one man's invention
changed the way people communicate.*

Facts to Share ★

In the 1870's people communicated over long distances by sending telegraph
messages or mailing letters. But Alexander Graham Bell thought he could
improve long-distance communication by inventing a way to send a person's
voice through a wire. He invented and patented his first telephone—which
he called an "electrical speech machine"—in 1876. The following year, he
formed the Bell Telephone Company.

Introducing the Activity ★

Share the facts (above and at right) about Alexander Graham Bell. Then
invite children to tell about the different kinds of telephones that they use.
If desired, you might collect and display several different kinds of models,
such as dial, touchtone, and cell phones. Finally, have children make these
booklets to learn about how Bell's invention has changed over time.

Materials

For each child:
★ booklet patterns
  (pages 50–52)
★ scissors
★ glue
★ crayons

What to Do ★

1. Cut out the booklet patterns.

2. Glue page 1 to page 2 where indicated. Then glue page 4 to page 5.

3. Color the cover and write your name on the line.

4. Color the picture on each page. On page 7, write the year at the top of the
   page. Then draw a picture of the kind of phone you use.

5. Accordion-fold the booklet so that the cover is on top.

6. Read the booklet together, unfolding it one page at a time. Then pair up
   children and have them read their booklets to each other.

More Facts About . . .
Alexander Graham Bell
(1847–1922)

• Like his father, he taught deaf people.

• He made his first successful "phone
  call" to his assistant, Thomas Watson,
  who was in another room. In that call,
  he said, "Mr. Watson, come here, I
  want you!"

• He helped design a kite that could
  carry a person!

• He did scientific experiments and
  worked on inventions throughout
  his life.

• He died when he was 75 years old.

Taking It Further ★

Make picture cards for this activity that helps children understand how
telephones have changed over time. First copy the booklet pages 2–6,
color and cut out each of the phone pictures, then glue it to an index card.
Next, glue a magazine cutout of a cell phone to an additional card. For self-
checking purposes, number the back of the cards from 1 to 6 to show the
order in which the phones evolved. Finally, place the cards in random order
in a pocket chart. To use, have children sequence the phones from earliest to
latest styles. As they work, encourage them to compare the different kinds
of phones.

Book Break ★

Alexander Graham Bell by Wil Mara (Children's Press, 2002). This book is
filled with historic photos illustrating information about Bell's life.

George Washington
Carver:

An
Amazing
Scientist

by _____

Materials

For each child:
★ booklet patterns
  (pages 53–54)
★ scissors
★ crayons
★ glue

To share:
★ stapler

More Facts About . . .
George Washington Carver
(1864–1943)

• As a child, he tended his own little garden in a nearby wood.

• He was nicknamed "The Plant Doctor" because he made medicine from plants.

• His research and discoveries helped poor farmers take care of the land and earn a good living.

• He discovered more than 300 uses for peanuts in his lifetime!

• In 1990—years after his death—he was inducted into The National Inventor's Hall of Fame.

George Washington Carver

*Children learn about a scientist who taught
farmers new ways to grow crops.*

Facts to Share ★★★★★★★★★★★★★★★★★★★★★★★★★★★★★

From an early age, George Washington Carver loved observing and learning about plants. When he was around 11 years old, he moved from home to attend school. He worked on a farm to pay for his education. After high school, he went to college and then became a teacher. In 1897, he was offered a job at the Tuskegee Institute in Alabama where he did research and developed a crop-rotation system that helped farmers grow better and larger crops. Carver also discovered many uses for plants such as peanuts, soybeans, and sweet potatoes.

Introducing the Activity ★★★★★★★★★★★★★★★★★★★★★★★★

Ask children to suggest ways that a scientist might help farmers. Explain that scientists can help farmers learn about ways to take care of the soil, grow healthy plants, and manage pests without poison. Then share facts (above and at left) to introduce children to a scientist who spent his life helping farmers—George Washington Carver. Afterward, invite them to make these booklets to share with family and friends.

What to Do ★★★★★★★★★★★★★★★★★★★★★★★★★★★★★★★★★

1. Cut out the booklet backing, cover, pages, and pictures boxes.

2. Color the backing and picture boxes. Write your name on the cover.

3. Read the text on pages 2–6. For each page, find the picture that matches the text. Glue that picture box to the page where indicated.

4. Sequence the pages, stack them behind the cover, and staple them to the backing where indicated.

5. Read the booklet together. Then form small groups and have children share their booklets with each other.

Taking It Further ★★★★★★★★★★★★★★★★★★★★★★★★★★★★★★

Conduct a taste-test using products made from one of George Washington Carver's favorite crops—soybeans! Set out small servings of up to four soybean food products, such as dry roasted soybeans, soy-based crackers, a sweet soy snack food, and cooked edamame (cooled to taste). Invite children to taste each food, and indicate whether they like it by drawing a tally mark next to "Yes" or "No" on a chart labeled with the food names. Afterward, review and compare the results on the chart. (Note: Check for food allergies before doing this activity.)

Book Break ★★★★★★★★★★★★★★★★★★★★★★★★★★★★★★★★★

George Washington Carver by Lynea Bowdish (Children's Press, 2004). This easy reader offers interesting facts about Carver's life and work.

Grandma Moses

*Children learn about an artist who
started her painting career at age 76!*

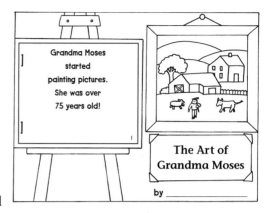

Facts to Share ★★★★★★★★★★★★★★★★★★★★★★★★★★★★★★★★★★

Anna Mary Robertson Moses lived and worked on farms her whole life. She
met her husband on a farm, helped him run a farm, and raised five children
on a farm. After her children moved away and her husband died, Mary
started painting pictures of farms and other landscapes. She was 76 years old
at the time! Over her lifetime, she painted more than 1,000 pictures, having
created 25 of these after her 100th birthday. Grandma Moses was 101 years
old when she died.

Introducing the Activity ★★★★★★★★★★★★★★★★★★★★★★★★★★★

After sharing facts about Grandma Moses (above and at right), read a book
to children about this inspirational artist (see Book Break). Discuss the kind
of places she painted as well as her painting style. Help children understand
that people loved her paintings because of their simplicity. Then invite
children to make these booklets about Grandma Moses.

What to Do ★★★★★★★★★★★★★★★★★★★★★★★★★★★★★★★★★★★★

1. Cut out the booklet backing and pages.

2. Stack the pages in sequence. Then staple them to the backing where
   indicated.

3. Read the text on each page. Draw a picture to match the text on
   pages 2–5.

4. Color the picture on the backing. Write your name on the line.

5. Read the booklet together. Then form small groups and have children
   share their booklets with each other.

Taking It Further ★★★★★★★★★★★★★★★★★★★★★★★★★★★★★★★

Break out the paints, set up easels, and invite students to paint pictures to
help create a landscape in the style of Grandma Moses. First, have children
paint a house, barn, farm animal, or tree. After their painting dries, help
them cut it out and add it to a bulletin board that's been covered with paper
to create green hills, a blue sky, and white clouds. Later, you might add word
cards to label all the pictures in the scene.

Book Break ★★★★★★★★★★★★★★★★★★★★★★★★★★★★★★★★★★★★

The Life and Works of Grandma Moses by Adam Schaefer (Heinemann Library,
2003). Reproductions of Grandma Moses' paintings illustrate this beginner
biography.

Materials

For each child:
★ booklet patterns
  (pages 55–56)
★ scissors
★ crayons

To share:
★ stapler

★ More Facts About . . . Grandma Moses
(1860–1961)

• She was the third of ten children.

• She went to a one-room country school
  and only attended during the summer.

• She took up painting after her arthritis
  forced her to give up embroidery.

• She was not a trained artist—she taught
  herself how to paint.

• She painted five to six hours a day, even
  though she was over 70 years old.

• Her art was very popular and some
  pieces were made into Christmas cards.

A Little Book About
Laura Ingalls Wilder

by _____

Word
List
frame
sod
life
log

Laura Ingalls Wilder

Children learn about an author who grew up living in little pioneer houses.

Facts to Share ★★★★★★★★★★★★★★★★★★★★★★★★★★★★★★★★★★

Laura Ingalls Wilder and her pioneer family moved many times during her early years. Some of the different kinds of homes that Wilder lived in included a little log house in the woods, a sod house on the prairie, and a two-story frame house in town. After living in Wisconsin, Kansas, Minnesota, and Iowa, the family finally settled in South Dakota in a little prairie town called DeSmet, where Wilder met her future husband and later began writing her popular books.

Introducing the Activity ★★★★★★★★★★★★★★★★★★★★★★★★★★★★

After sharing facts (above and at left) about Laura Ingalls Wilder, explain that her family built their log, sod, and frame houses from the ground up, using materials found at the home sites. Talk about what kinds of materials and tools they might have needed to build each house. Also discuss the difficulties they might have had building a home without a hardware or supply store nearby. Then have children "build" these cabin-shaped booklets to share with their family and friends.

Materials

For each child:
★ booklet patterns (pages 57–59)
★ scissors
★ pencil
★ crayons

To share:
★ stapler

What to Do ★★★★★★★★★★★★★★★★★★★★★★★★★★★★★★★★★★★

1. Cut out the booklet backing, cover, and pages.

2. Sequence the pages, stack them behind the cover, and staple them to the backing where indicated.

3. Read the word list on the cover. Then read pages 1–4. Choose a word from the list that best completes the text on the page. Write that word on the line. (Answers: 1. *life*, 2. *log*, 3. *sod*, 4. *frame*)

4. Draw a picture to go with the sentence on each page.

5. Color the cover and backing. Write your name on the line.

6. Read the booklet together. Then form small groups and have children share their booklets with each other.

More Facts About . . .
Laura Ingalls Wilder
(1867–1957)

- She got her teaching certificate when she was 15 years old.

- She married Almanzo Wilder, and they later moved to Mansfield, Missouri, where they built a home and named it Rocky Ridge.

- Her daughter, Rose, encouraged her to write a story about her childhood.

- At the age of 65, her first book—about her experiences and life on the frontier—was published!

- She lived at Rocky Ridge Farm for more than 60 years—until she died at the age of 90.

Taking It Further ★★★★★★★★★★★★★★★★★★★★★★★★★★★★★★

Invite children to write little books about their own family life. To make a booklet, stack two sheets of paper, fold in half, and staple along the left side (folded side). Then ask children to draw a picture of their home on the cover and help them title their booklets "A Little Book About My Home." On each of the inside pages, have children write something about their family life and then illustrate their text. Encourage them to share their completed booklets with classmates.

Book Break ★★★★★★★★★★★★★★★★★★★★★★★★★★★★★★★★★★

Laura Ingalls Wilder by Wil Mara (Children's Press, 2003). Wilder's life and work is featured in this beginner biography.

The Little House Guidebook by William Anderson (HarperTrophy, 1966). Features information, photos, and maps for every place that the Ingalls family called home.

Helen Keller

*Children learn about a deaf and blind woman
who let nothing stop her from learning.*

Facts to Share ★★★★★★★★★★★★★★★★★★★★★★★★★★★★★

When Helen Keller was 19 months old, she developed an illness that left her deaf and blind. Her parents hired Anne Sullivan to be her live-in teacher when Keller was six years old. Before long, she learned how to use finger spelling to communicate with others. She later learned to read and write Braille, to lip-read through touch, and to speak! Keller went to college, began a writing career, traveled, and gave speeches around the world. She was an advocate for the deaf and blind population her entire life.

Introducing the Activity ★★★★★★★★★★★★★★★★★★★★★★★★

Share facts (above and at right) about Helen Keller. Then invite children to tell about some of their own difficulties in learning new things at school or home and how they overcame any obstacles. You might also share about some of your own experiences. Finally, have children make these informational booklets about Helen Keller and her accomplishments.

What to Do ★★★★★★★★★★★★★★★★★★★★★★★★★★★★★★★★

1. Color and cut out the booklet cover, pages, and word boxes.

2. Sequence the pages, stack them behind the cover, and staple them to the backing where indicated.

3. Read pages 1–6. For each page, find the word that completes the sentence. Glue that word box to the page where indicated.

4. Color the picture on the backing. Write your name on the cover.

5. Read the booklet together. Then form small groups and have children share their booklets with each other.

Taking It Further ★★★★★★★★★★★★★★★★★★★★★★★★★★★★

Helen Keller was an excellent typist, even though she could not see. To help children understand how difficult typing words without sight might be, invite them to type a few easy three-letter words on the computer. Then ask them to close their eyes or put on a blindfold and retype the same words. When finished, have children check the screen to compare each set of words. How did they do? Discuss whether or not being sightless made typing the words more difficult.

Book Break ★★★★★★★★★★★★★★★★★★★★★★★★★★★★★★★

Helen Keller by Pamela Walker (Children's Press, 2001). This is a very simple, photo-illustrated, emergent reader biography.

Helen Keller by Sean Dolan (Children's Press, 2005). This book is loaded with historical photos documenting Keller's life.

Materials

For each child:
★ booklet patterns
  (pages 60–62)
★ scissors
★ glue
★ crayons

To share:
★ stapler

★ More Facts About . . . Helen Keller
(1880–1968)

• The first word that she understood through finger spelling was *water*.

• At age 22, she published her autobiography called *The Story of My Life*.

• She took part in the campaign to give women the right to vote.

• She traveled to 39 countries around the world.

• She received the Presidential Medal of Freedom in 1964.

• She loved dogs and was the first American owner of an Akita, which was a gift from the Japanese.

by _____

Materials

For each child:
★ booklet patterns (pages 63–65)
★ scissors
★ glue
★ crayons

To share:
★ stapler

More Facts About . . . Jim Thorpe
(1888–1953)

• He was coached by Pop Warner at the Carlisle School, where he scored 25 touchdowns his last year there.

• He played major and minor league baseball for 20 years.

• He played for three different major league baseball teams: the New York Giants, Cincinnati Reds, and Boston Braves

• He played professional football until age 41!

• Jim Thorpe, Pennsylvania was named in honor of him.

Jim Thorpe

Children learn about a Native American who became an amazing athlete.

Facts to Share ★

Jim Thorpe, a Native American from Oklahoma, went to a strict boarding school at the age of six. When he was 14, he enrolled in a school for Native American students in Carlisle, Pennsylvania, where he joined the track and field, football, and baseball teams. He excelled at track and field events so much so that he took part in the 1912 Olympics, winning gold medals in the pentathlon and decathlon! In 1950, Thorpe was named the greatest American athlete of the first half of the twentieth century.

Introducing the Activity ★

After sharing facts (above and at left) about Jim Thorpe, explain that a pentathlon includes five combined events: a 200-meter sprint, 1500-meter race, long jump, javelin throw, and discus throw. The decathlon includes the last four events listed for the pentathlon plus a 100-meter sprint, 400-meter race, 110-meter hurdles, shot put, high jump, and pole vault. Describe each event and discuss the skills and strength that Thorpe must have possessed to win gold medals in each competition. Then have children make these booklets about his athletic skills.

What to Do ★

1. Cut out the booklet backing, cover, pages, and pictures.

2. Sequence the pages, stack them behind the cover, and staple them to the backing where indicated.

3. Read pages 1–4. For each page, find the picture that matches the text. Glue that picture to the page where indicated.

4. Draw the two gold medals on page 5.

5. Color the pages and backing. Write your name on the line on the backing.

6. Read the booklet together. Then form small groups and have children share their booklets with each other.

Taking It Further ★

Tell children that in addition to football, baseball, and track and field, Jim Thorpe also excelled in basketball, lacrosse, ice hockey, tennis, archery, boxing, and swimming! Have children draw a picture of themselves participating in a sport or other activity that interests them and then write (or dictate) sentences to describe ways that they might be successful in that activity. Bind their completed pages together to create a class book titled "On Our Way to Success!"

Book Break ★

Young Jim Thorpe, Bright Path by Don Brown (Square Fish, 2006). Action-filled watercolor art illustrates Jim's path from childhood to the 1912 Olympics.

Amelia Earhart

Children learn about a record-breaking female pilot who inspired the world!

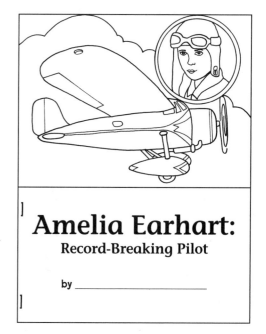

Amelia Earhart:
Record-Breaking Pilot

by _____

Facts to Share ★★★★★★★★★★★★★★★★★★★★★★★★★★★★★★

Amelia Earhart began flying lessons at age 21. Over her career, she broke seven women's speed and distance flying records, became the first female to fly solo across the Atlantic Ocean, and was the first person to fly across both the Atlantic and Pacific oceans. In addition to flying planes, Earhart wrote books and magazine articles about flying and went on lecture tours encouraging women to become pilots. Her many accomplishments made her a worldwide celebrity.

Introducing the Activity ★★★★★★★★★★★★★★★★★★★★★★★★★

After sharing facts (above and at right) about Amelia Earhart, invite children to tell about something they'd like to do that no one has done before. Discuss the possible obstacles they might encounter in being "first" to accomplish their goal. Then ask them to name some obstacles they think Earhart may have faced. Finally, have children make these booklets about her aviation accomplishments.

What to Do ★★★★★★★★★★★★★★★★★★★★★★★★★★★★★★★★★

1. Cut out the booklet backing, cover, and pages.

2. Sequence the pages, stack them behind the cover, and staple them to the backing where indicated.

3. Read and color pages 1–4. On page 4, draw a picture of yourself as a pilot.

4. Color the picture on the backing. Then write your name on the cover.

5. Read the booklet together. Then form small groups and have children share their booklets with each other.

Taking It Further ★★★★★★★★★★★★★★★★★★★★★★★★★★★★★★

Create a classroom aviation mural by covering a bulletin board with blue paper to represent the sky. Add large white paper cloud cutouts. Then prepare for each child a large sheet of drawing paper with "If I flew an airplane, I would fly to (name of a place)." Have children write (or dictate) an ending to the sentence and then illustrate it. Display the pages on the bulletin board along with the title "Aviation Dreams Inspired by Amelia."

Book Break ★★★★★★★★★★★★★★★★★★★★★★★★★★★★★★★★★

Amelia Earhart by Philip Abraham (Children's Press, 2002). This is a simple, photo-illustrated emergent reader biography of Amelia Earhart.

Amelia Earhart by Wil Mara (Children's Press, 2002). This book is filled with historical photos documenting Earhart's life.

Materials

For each child:
- ★ booklet patterns (pages 66–68)
- ★ scissors
- ★ crayons

To share:
- ★ stapler

More Facts About . . .
Amelia Earhart
(1897–1937)

- When she was young, she enjoyed reading books and poetry, but also loved sports, including football, baseball, and fishing.

- She nursed soldiers injured in World War I.

- She named one of her planes "Old Bessie, the Fire Horse."

- She helped start a club for women pilots called the "Ninety Nines."

- Her plane disappeared in 1937 while she was making an around-the-world flight.

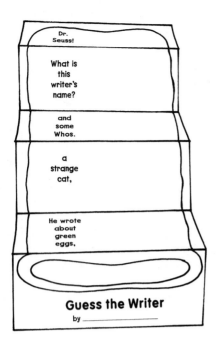

Guess the Writer
by _____

Materials

For each child:
★ booklet patterns
   (pages 69–70)
★ scissors
★ glue
★ crayons

More Facts About . . .
Dr. Seuss
(1904–1991)

• His first book was rejected 27 times
before finally being accepted by a
publisher.

• He wrote *The Cat in the Hat* as an
agreement with his publisher to write
a book using only 225 early-reader
vocabulary words.

• He used only fifty different words in
writing *Green Eggs and Ham*.

• He wrote 44 books in all

• He has won a number of awards for
his books, including three Caldecott
Honor awards.

• His books have been translated into
15 different languages.

Dr. Seuss

Children learn about an author and his world of imagination.

Facts to Share ★★★★★★★★★★★★★★★★★★★★★★★★★★★★★★★

Dr. Seuss's real name was Theodore Seuss Geisel. As a student at Dartmouth
College, he wrote articles for the college newspaper and magazine. He also
enjoyed drawing and, after touring Europe, he returned to the United States
to began working on a career as a cartoonist. Geisel was good at making up
rhymes. He combined his rhyming and drawing talents to create his first
book, *And to Think That I Saw It on Mulberry Street*. In 1957, he published
The Cat in the Hat, which was so popular that it made him a successful
children's book author and illustrator!

Introducing the Activity ★★★★★★★★★★★★★★★★★★★★★★★★

Share facts (above and at left) about Dr. Seuss. Then name a few of his
characters, such as Loraxes, Sneetches, and the Grinch. Invite children to
share what they know about these and other Seussian characters. Conclude
the discussion by telling them that Dr. Seuss used his talent for creating
rhymes and whimsical art to help make reading fun for kids of all ages.
Then have children make these foldout booklets that includes a few of his
character creations.

What to Do ★★★★★★★★★★★★★★★★★★★★★★★★★★★★★★★★★

1. Cut out the booklet patterns.

2. Glue page 2 to page 3 where indicated.

3. Write your name on the line.

4. Read each page. Then draw a picture to match the text.

5. Accordion-fold the booklet so that the cover is on top.

6. Read the booklet together, unfolding it one page at a time to create a
   tall hat. Later, pair up children and have them read their booklets to
   each other.

Taking It Further ★★★★★★★★★★★★★★★★★★★★★★★★★★★★★

Challenge children to list as many Dr. Seuss characters as possible. Write
their responses on chart paper. Then invite them to draw their favorite
character from the list on a 9- by 12-inch sheet of white construction paper.
Have children write (or dictate) their character's name on the back of their
paper as well as on a sentence strip. Place the pictures and name strips in a
center for children to match. They can check their work by looking at the
name on the back of the pictures.

Book Break ★★★★★★★★★★★★★★★★★★★★★★★★★★★★★★★★★

Dr. Seuss by Dana Meachen Rau (Children's Press, 2003). Pictures of Dr. Seuss
and his famous characters animate the pages of this beginner biography.

Rachel Carson

*Children learn about a nature writer
who helped to protect our environment.*

Facts to Share ★★★★★★★★★★★★★★★★★★★★★★★★★★★★★★★★

Rachel Carson loved to write and explore nature as a young girl. In college,
she studied English, biology, and writing and then combined her education
and writing skills to pursue a career as a scientist and editor. Carson got a
job with the government, writing materials about plants, animals, and their
environments. In 1962, she published a book about how pesticides were
harmful to animals, humans, and the environment. Through her research
and writings, Carson inspired ecological awareness and helped get laws
passed to protect the environment.

Introducing the Activity ★★★★★★★★★★★★★★★★★★★★★★★★★★

Share facts (above and at right) about Rachel Carson and point out that she
observed nature. Ask children to tell what *observe* means and what they
might learn by observing nature. Explain that by careful observation and
study, Carson discovered things that harmed the environment. Afterward,
have children make these booklets to share with family and friends.

What to Do ★★★★★★★★★★★★★★★★★★★★★★★★★★★★★★★★★★★

1. Cut out the booklet backing, cover, pages, and word boxes.

2. Color the backing. Write your name on the cover.

3. Read pages 1–7. For each page, find the word that matches the picture
   and completes the sentence. Glue that word box to the page where
   indicated.

4. Write an ending to the sentence on page 8. Then draw a picture.

5. Sequence the pages, stack them behind the cover, and staple them to the
   backing where indicated.

6. Read the booklet together. Then form small groups and have children
   share their booklets with each other.

Taking It Further ★★★★★★★★★★★★★★★★★★★★★★★★★★★★★★★

Take children outdoors to observe plants, insects, animals, and birds. After
returning to the classroom, discuss their observations. Write some of the
items they name along the left side of a sheet of chart paper. Then work with
children to compose sentences that describe each item. Write the sentences
next to the words and then review the sentences, pointing out that each one
begins with a capital letter and ends with punctuation. Later, invite children
to copy a few sentences onto paper and illustrate them.

Book Break ★★★★★★★★★★★★★★★★★★★★★★★★★★★★★★★★★★★

Rachel Carson by Justine and Ron Fontes (Children's Press, 2005). Simple
text and interesting photos tell the story of this ground-breaking scientist.

Materials

For each child:
★ booklet patterns
  (pages 71–73)
★ scissors
★ crayons
★ glue

To share:
★ stapler

More Facts About . . . Rachel Carson

(1907–1964)

• She was born and grew up on a farm in
  Pennsylvania.

• She wrote a story for a magazine when
  she was only 10!

• She went underwater in a diving suit to
  study fish.

• She worked for the U.S. Bureau of
  Fisheries, which is now the U.S. Fish
  and Wildlife Service.

• Her second book, *The Sea Around
  Us*, became a bestseller and has been
  translated into 32 languages.

Rosa Parks

by _____

Materials

For each child:
★ booklet patterns
   (pages 74–75)
★ scissors
★ glue
★ crayons

To share:
★ stapler

More Facts About . . . Rosa Parks

(1913–2005)

• She attended segregated schools in Alabama.

• She worked as a seamstress at the time she was arrested.

• She participated in the 382-day Montgomery bus boycott that was led by Martin Luther King, Jr.

• In 1996, President Clinton awarded her the Congressional Medal of Honor.

• She received a Congressional Gold Medal in 1999.

• She lived to be 92 years old!

Rosa Parks

Children learn about a courageous woman who fought for civil rights.

Facts to Share ★★★★★★★★★★★★★★★★★★★★★★★★★★★★★★★

In 1955, Rosa Parks was arrested for refusing to give up her seat on a bus to a white passenger. Her brave act helped launch the bus boycott in Montgomery, Alabama, which eventually led to the passage of civil rights laws. Parks worked her entire life to promote equality for all by traveling and speaking to groups about civil rights. After her husband died, she founded the Rosa and Raymond Parks Institute for Self-Development, an organization that educates young people about the history of the country and civil rights movement.

Introducing the Activity ★★★★★★★★★★★★★★★★★★★★★★★★★★

After sharing facts (above and at left) about Rosa Parks, write her name across the top of a sheet of chart paper. Along the left side, list the words *who*, *where*, *what*, and *how*, leaving space next to and below each word to write sentences. Then invite children to share what they know about this courageous woman. You might ask them to tell who she was, where she lived, what she did, and how she helped others. Write their responses on the chart next to the most appropriate word. Review the information on the chart, then invite children to make these lift-the-flap booklets about Rosa Parks.

What to Do ★★★★★★★★★★★★★★★★★★★★★★★★★★★★★★★★★★

1. Cut out the booklet backing, cover, pages, and flaps.

2. Color the backing. Write your name on the cover.

3. Read pages 1–4. For each page, find the flap labeled with the question that can be answered by the text. Glue that flap to the page where indicated.

4. Sequence the pages, stack them behind the cover, and staple them to the backing where indicated.

5. To use, have children read the question on each flap and then lift the flap to read the answer.

Taking It Further ★★★★★★★★★★★★★★★★★★★★★★★★★★★★★★

Invite children to draw a picture of something they learned about Rosa Parks. Have them write (or dictate) a sentence to describe their picture. Then collect the completed pages and bind them together to create a class book titled "Rosa Parks: Standing Firm for Freedom."

Book Break ★★★★★★★★★★★★★★★★★★★★★★★★★★★★★★★★★★

I Am Rosa Parks by Rosa Parks (Puffin, 1999). In her autobiography, Parks describes her experiences during the Montgomery Bus Boycott.

Rosa Parks by Wil Mara (Children's Press, 2005). Young children learn about the life and work of this courageous civil rights activist.

Jackie Robinson

Children learn about the first African-American major league baseball player.

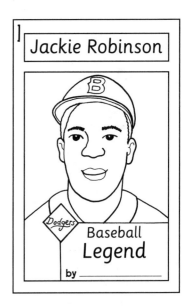

Facts to Share ★★★★★★★★★★★★★★★★★★★★★★★★★★★★★★★★★★★

At his college, Jackie Robinson was the first player to be awarded a varsity letter in four sports: baseball, basketball, football, and track. After leaving college, he became a second lieutenant in the army. He was court-martialed when he refused to move to the back of a segregated bus, but received an honorable discharge before he left the Army. He then began a career as a professional baseball player, becoming the first African American to play major league baseball. After retiring from baseball, Robinson worked in many ways to help African Americans overcome barriers to success.

Introducing the Activity ★★★★★★★★★★★★★★★★★★★★★★★★★★★★★

Invite children to name their favorite baseball players and tell why they are special. Then ask if they have ever heard of Jackie Robinson. Encourage them to share what they know about this inspirational baseball player. Next, share facts (above and at right) about Robinson and discuss his contributions to baseball and the civil rights movement. Finally, have children make these unique booklets about Jackie Robinson.

Materials

For each child:
★ booklet patterns (pages 76–78)
★ scissors
★ crayons

To share:
★ stapler

What to Do ★★★★★★★★★★★★★★★★★★★★★★★★★★★★★★★★★★★★

1. Cut out the booklet cover and pages.

2. Color the border around each page. Then follow these directions to complete each page:

   cover: Color the picture. Write your name on the line.

   page 1: Draw a baseball inside the diamond.

   page 2: Color the *B* blue.

   page 3: Draw a baseball base on each corner of the diamond.

   page 4: Color the number.

   page 5: Draw a baseball player inside the diamond.

3. Sequence and stack the pages behind the cover. Staple them together in the upper left corner.

4. Read the booklet together. Then form small groups and have children share their booklets with each other.

More Facts About . . . Jackie Robinson
(1919–1972)

• In 1947, his first year of playing major league baseball, he was selected as Rookie of the Year.

• He was named the National League's Most Valuable Player in 1949.

• He was inducted into the Baseball Hall of Fame in 1962.

• His uniform number, 42, was the first to be retired by all teams.

• He was the first professional baseball player to be featured on a stamp.

Taking It Further ★★★★★★★★★★★★★★★★★★★★★★★★★★★★★★

Gather inexpensive baseball cards to use in this activity. (You might request donations or purchase cards from a thrift shop). Tell children that Jackie Robinson was featured on a number of baseball cards. Explain that the cards gave both fun and important information about him. Display a few baseball cards in a pocket chart. Invite children to choose a card and then use it to share information about that player with the class (such as the player's name, team, uniform number, and birthday).

Book Break ★★★★★★★★★★★★★★★★★★★★★★★★★★★★★★★★★★

Jackie Robinson by Philip Abraham (Children's Press, 2002). This photo-illustrated book highlights Robinson's history-making baseball career.

Cesar Chavez:
A Man Who
Cared
by _____

Cesar Chavez helped
farm
workers.

Materials

For each child:
★ booklet patterns
  (pages 79–81)
★ scissors
★ crayons

To share:
★ stapler

More Facts About . . .
Cesar Chavez
(1927–1993)

• He left school after 8th grade to help his family.

• He joined the Navy and served in World War II.

• He inspired the public to boycott grapes until workers' conditions improved.

• His lifelong motto was "It can be done."

• In 1994—after his death—President Clinton awarded him the Congressional Medal of Honor.

Cesar Chavez

Children learn about a man who fought for the rights of farm workers.

Facts to Share ★★★★★★★★★★★★★★★★★★★★★★★★★★★★★★★★★★★★

When Cesar Chavez was young, his Mexican-American family owned an Arizona farm and grocery store. During the Depression, they had to sell their property due to financial hardships. They then moved from farm to farm looking for work picking fruits and vegetables. His experience as a migrant farm worker led Chavez to try to improve the lives of farm workers. He organized the United Farm Workers, a group that held protests, strikes, and boycotts in an effort to get better housing, pay, and working conditions for field workers.

Introducing the Activity ★★★★★★★★★★★★★★★★★★★★★★★★★★★★★★

After sharing facts (above and at left) about Cesar Chavez, work with children to come up with words or phrases that describe some things that he helped to change for farm workers, such as *housing*, *pay*, *education*, and *working conditions*. Write their responses on chart paper. Then review the list and discuss how Chavez's work helped to improve the lives of farm workers. Afterward, invite children to make these booklets to share with family and friends.

What to Do ★★★★★★★★★★★★★★★★★★★★★★★★★★★★★★★★★★★★★★★

1. Cut out the booklet backing, cover, pages, and word boxes.

2. Follow these directions to complete each page:

   cover: Write your name on the line.

   pages 1, 3, and 5: Find the word that completes the sentence on each page. Glue that word box to the page where indicated.

   pages 2, 4, and 6: Draw a picture according to the directions.

   page 7 and backing: Trace the words to complete the sentence. Then color the backing and write your name on the author line.

3. Sequence the pages, stack them behind the cover, and staple them to the backing where indicated.

4. Read the booklet together. Then form small groups and have children share their booklets with each other.

Taking It Further ★★★★★★★★★★★★★★★★★★★★★★★★★★★★★★★★★★★

Ask children to share why farm workers are important to everyone. List their ideas in the center of a sheet of chart paper, leaving wide margins around the edges. After reviewing the list, invite children to draw fruits and vegetables in the area around the listed words to create a colorful border. Then display the chart with the title "Farm Workers Are Fabulous!"

Book Break ★★★★★★★★★★★★★★★★★★★★★★★★★★★★★★★★★★★★★★★

Cesar Chavez by Susan Eddy (Children's Press, 2003). Simple text and photographs tell the story of this Hispanic-American civil rights worker.

Dr. Martin Luther King, Jr.

*Children learn about a man who worked
for equality for all Americans.*

Facts to Share ★★★★★★★★★★★★★★★★★★★★★★★★★★★★★★★★★★

Dr. Martin Luther King, Jr. lived in Alabama during a time when African
Americans had to go to separate schools, ride in the back of buses, and even
drink from separate water fountains. He worked to win equal treatment for
his children and all people by organizing nonviolent protests and marches.
In 1963, he delivered his famous "I Have a Dream" speech to 250,000 people
in Washington, D.C. His work and speeches inspired many and led to the
passage of the Civil Rights Act in 1964.

Introducing the Activity ★★★★★★★★★★★★★★★★★★★★★★★★★★★★

After sharing facts (above and at right) about Dr. Martin Luther King, Jr.,
discuss the difference between a dream that occurs during sleep and one that
represents hope for the future. Invite children to share their dreams for the
future. Then explain that Dr. King's dream was for *all* Americans to be treated
equally. Finally, have them make these 3-D booklets about Dr. King's dream.

What to Do ★★★★★★★★★★★★★★★★★★★★★★★★★★★★★★★★★★★★

1. Cut out the booklet backing and flaps.

2. Color the backing and write your name on the line.

3. Glue the top, right, and left flaps to the backing where indicated. Glue each
   flap facedown. Then fold it back so that it is face up. When all the flaps are
   folded back, they will resemble a large speech bubble.

4. With the flaps folded back, read the text and complete the booklet by doing
   the following:
   - Draw four children in the box at the top of the right flap.
   - Color the map on the top flap.
   - Color the hand at the bottom of the right flap.

5. To close the booklet, fold down the left and right flaps along the light gray
   line. Then close the left, right, and top flaps, in that order.

6. To use, have children fold back all of the flaps and read the text.

Taking It Further ★★★★★★★★★★★★★★★★★★★★★★★★★★★★★★★

Invite children to share their dreams for the future. First, write "I have a
dream to . . ." on a class supply of 12- by 18-inch white construction paper.
Have children write (or dictate) an ending to the sentence and illustrate it.
Then bind the pages into a class book titled "Our Dreams for the Future."

Book Break ★★★★★★★★★★★★★★★★★★★★★★★★★★★★★★★★★★★

Martin Luther King, Jr. by Wil Mara (Children's Press, 2005). Inspiring
historical photos illustrate the life and work of an important civil rights leader.

Materials

For each child:
★ booklet patterns
  (pages 82–84)
★ scissors
★ glue
★ crayons

More Facts About . . .
Dr. Martin Luther King, Jr.
(1929–1968)

- He started college at age 15.
- He wanted to be a medical doctor,
  but he earned a doctorate degree in
  Theology instead.
- In 1964, at age 35, he became the
  youngest man to receive the Nobel
  Peace Prize.
- The nation mourned his death when
  he was assassinated in 1968.
- January 15 is a national holiday set
  aside to honor the anniversary of
  Dr. King's birth.

Wilma Rudolph:
Sprinting
Star
by
_____

by _____

Materials

For each child:
* booklet patterns (pages 85–87)
* scissors
* glue
* crayons

To share:
* stapler

More Facts About . . . Wilma Rudolph
(1940–1994)

• She was nicknamed "Skeeter" for being little, fast, and in the way!

• She set a state high school basketball record for scoring the most points in one game.

• After retiring from competition, she returned to college and became a teacher and athletic coach.

• She created The Wilma Rudolph Foundation to help young athletes.

• She was inducted into the U.S. Olympic Hall of Fame in 1983.

• In 2004, the U.S. Postal Service issued a postage stamp in recognition of her accomplishments.

Wilma Rudolph

*Children learn about a determined athlete
who went the distance for Olympic gold.*

Facts to Share ★★★★★★★★★★★★★★★★★★★★★★★★★★★★★★★★★

From the moment of her premature birth, Wilma Rudolph had to fight to overcome health problems. Then, at age 4, she contracted polio and had to wear leg braces. At nine years old, she was able to take off her braces and walk! From then on, she enjoyed running, jumping, and especially playing basketball. During the summers of her high school years, she trained with a college track team. When she was 16, Rudolph won a bronze medal in the 1956 Melbourne Olympics. Four years later, she won three gold medals at the 1960 Rome Olympics!

Introducing the Activity ★★★★★★★★★★★★★★★★★★★★★★★★★★★★

After sharing facts (above and at left) about Wilma Rudolph, draw a large Olympic Rings symbol on the board, leaving space inside the rings for writing. Add the heading "What it takes to be an Olympic athlete." Explain what the symbol represents and then invite children to describe what it takes to become an Olympic athlete. Write their responses inside the rings. After discussing, have them make these booklets about Wilma Rudolph.

What to Do ★★★★★★★★★★★★★★★★★★★★★★★★★★★★★★★★★★★★

1. Cut out the booklet backing, cover, pages, title box, and word boxes.

2. Sequence the pages, stack them behind the cover, and staple them to the backing where indicated.

3. Glue the title box to the backing where indicated. Then color the backing and write your name on the line.

4. Read pages 1–6. For each page, find the word that best completes the sentence. Glue that word box to the page where indicated. (Answers: 1. *child*, 2. *strong*, 3. *ran*, 4. *Olympics*, 5. *races*, 6. *medals*)

5. Read the booklet together. Then form small groups and have children share their booklets with each other.

Taking It Further ★★★★★★★★★★★★★★★★★★★★★★★★★★★★★★★

Invite children to make gold medals for themselves! First, prepare for each child a large yellow construction paper circle with "(Child's name) is determined to work hard and (description of goal)." Have children complete the sentence with their name and a personal goal, and then decorate their medal with gold glitter. To complete, help them staple a red or blue crepe paper "ribbon" to the top.

Book Break ★★★★★★★★★★★★★★★★★★★★★★★★★★★★★★★★★★★

Wilma Unlimited: How Wilma Rudolph Became the World's Fastest Woman by Kathleen Krull (Voyager Books, 2000). Bright, bold illustrations highlight this book about Rudolph's childhood and her road to the Olympics.

Ellen Ochoa

Children learn about the world's first Hispanic female astronaut.

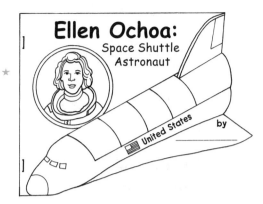

Ellen Ochoa:
Space Shuttle
Astronaut
United States   by

Facts to Share ★★★★★★★★★★★★★★★★★★★★★★★★★★★★★★★★★★★★

While in graduate school, Ellen Ochoa began to dream of taking part in a space flight. She applied to be an astronaut with NASA in 1985 and was selected as a final candidate in 1990. After completing a mentally and physically challenging training program, Ochoa officially became an astronaut in July, 1991 and participated in her first space shuttle mission in 1993. Altogether, she made four space shuttle flights and logged 978 hours in space!

Introducing the Activity ★★★★★★★★★★★★★★★★★★★★★★★★★★★★

Share a book about Ellen Ochoa (see "Book Break"). After reading, share additional facts (above and at right) about this fascinating woman. Then discuss the different things she did that helped her become an astronaut. Finally, tell children that Ochoa loved to visit schools to encourage students and let them know that her opportunities were the result of a good educational background. Then have them make these booklets to reinforce what they learned about this inspirational astronaut.

What to Do ★★

1. Cut out the booklet cover, picture, pages, and flaps.

2. Follow these directions to complete each page:

   cover: Glue the picture of Ochoa to the page. Color the picture and write your name on the line.

   page 1: Glue flaps A and B where indicated. Color the picture.

   page 2: Glue flaps C and D where indicated. Color the picture.

3. Sequence the pages, stack them behind the cover, and staple them together along the left edge.

4. To read the booklet, have children read the question on each flap. Then have them lift the flap to read the answer.

Taking It Further ★★★★★★★★★★★★★★★★★★★★★★★★★★★★★★★★★★★

Invite children to imagine what it must be like to be an astronaut. Afterward, have them make personalized booklets about their imaginary experiences. To prepare, mask the name Ellen Ochoa on a copy of the booklet cover (page 88) and then copy a class quantity of the cover. Have children cut out their cover and staple it to several 8½- by 6½-inch sheets of white paper. Ask them to write their name in the title and glue a copy of their school photo to the circle. Finally, have them complete their booklets with text and illustrations about their experiences.

Book Break ★★★★★★★★★★★★★★★★★★★★★★★★★★★★★★★★★★★★★★★

Ellen Ochoa by Elizabeth D. Jaffe (Children's Press, 2004). Young readers follow Ochoa's adventures in training to be an astronaut and making a space-shuttle flight.

Ellen Ochoa by Pam Walker (Children's Press, 2000). This photo-illustrated, emergent reader offers a simple biography of the world's first Hispanic female astronaut.

Materials

For each child:
★ booklet patterns (pages 88–90)
★ scissors
★ glue
★ crayons

To share:
★ stapler

More Facts About . . . Ellen Ochoa

(1958–)

• She was on the first shuttle flight to dock with the International Space Station.

• She was a crewmember twice on both the space shuttles *Discovery* and *Atlantis*.

• She became an expert at using the space shuttle's robotic arm in space!

• Over the years, she has also been successful as a researcher, scientist, inventor, airplane pilot, and flutist.

Barack Obama
44th President of the United States

by _____

Materials

For each child:
* ★ booklet patterns (pages 91–93)
* ★ scissors
* ★ crayons
* ★ glue
* ★ pencil

To share:
* ★ stapler

More Facts About . . .
Barack Obama
(1961–)

* He was born in Honolulu, Hawaii.
* At age 6, he moved to Indonesia and then returned to Hawaii when he was ten years old.
* He loved to play basketball in high school.
* In addition to his other occupations, he has taught college classes and written books.
* He became the 44th President of the United States.

Barack Obama

Children learn about the 44th President of the United States.

Facts to Share ★★★★★★★★★★★★★★★★★★★★★★★★★★★★★★★

From a young age, Barack Obama's family taught him that education and hard work could lead to a better life. He worked his way through college, with the aid of scholarships and student loans. While living in Illinois, he worked as a community organizer and lawyer before being elected a State Senator in 1996. He became a United States Senator for Illinois in 2005. Then, in 2008, Obama made history when he was elected the first African-American President of the United States!

Introducing the Activity ★★★★★★★★★★★★★★★★★★★★★★★★★★★

After sharing facts (above and at left) about Barack Obama, invite children to share what they know about how a person becomes the President of the United States, where the president lives, and what kind of work the president does for the country. Afterward, discuss the different symbols related to the president. Then invite students to make these booklets that highlight symbols of Barack Obama's presidency.

What to Do ★★★★★★★★★★★★★★★★★★★★★★★★★★★★★★★★★★★

1. Cut out the booklet backing, cover, pages, and symbol boxes.
2. Color the backing and symbols. Write your name on the cover.
3. Read pages 1–4. For each page, find the symbol that matches the text. Glue that symbol box to the page where indicated.
4. Trace the word on page 5.
5. Sequence the pages, stack them behind the cover, and staple them to the backing where indicated.
6. Read the booklet together. Then form small groups and have children share their booklets with each other.

Taking It Further ★★★★★★★★★★★★★★★★★★★★★★★★★★★★★★★★

When Barack Obama ran for president, he talked about his hope for people to work together to build a better country. One of his slogans was "Yes We Can!" Encourage children to work together to plan and complete a project—such as planting a garden or cleaning their workspace—to help make their classroom or school a better place.

Book Break ★★★★★★★★★★★★★★★★★★★★★★★★★★★★★★★★★★★

Barack Obama: United States President: Updated and Expanded by Roberta Edwards (Grosset & Dunlop, 2009). The campaign and election of Barack Obama is highlighted in this book for young readers.

Meet President Barack Obama by Laine Falk (Children's Press, 2009). This early learner title provides photos and simple information about our 44th president.

Kristi Yamaguchi

*Children learn about a graceful athlete
who skated her way to Olympic gold!*

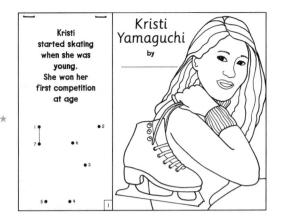

Facts to Share ★★★★★★★★★★★★★★★★★★★★★★★★★★★★★

As a baby, Kristi Yamaguchi wore leg casts and braces to correct a foot problem. She began dance lessons at age 4, but Kristi really wanted to ice skate. After she learned to read, she was allowed to start skating. Kristi worked hard at skating; it took a lot of her time, but she still did well in her studies. And although she didn't always win important competitions, she never gave up. Finally, in 1991, she won the World Championship. The next year, she won the U.S. Nationals and then a gold medal at the 1992 Albertville Olympics!

Introducing the Activity ★★★★★★★★★★★★★★★★★★★★★★★★★

Draw a KWL chart titled "Kristi Yamaguchi" on an oval-shaped sheet of white bulletin board paper. Invite children to share what they know and what they want to know about this famous skater. Record their responses on the chart. Then share facts (above and at right) about Yamaguchi. Afterward, discuss what children learned and add this information to the chart. Finally, have children make these connect-the-dot booklets to reinforce what they know about Kristi Yamaguchi.

Materials

For each child:
★ booklet patterns
  (pages 94–96)
★ scissors
★ crayons

To share:
★ stapler

What to Do ★★★★★★★★★★★★★★★★★★★★★★★★★★★★★★★★★

1. Cut out the booklet backing and pages.

2. Sequence the pages and staple them to the backing where indicated.

3. Connect the dots to complete each picture on pages 1–5. Then color the picture.

4. Color the backing and write your name on the line.

5. Read the booklet together. Then form small groups and have children share their booklets with each other.

More Facts About . . .
Kristi Yamaguchi
(1971–)

• After the 1992 Olympics, she toured for ten years as a professional skater with Stars on Ice.

• She was inducted into the U.S. Figure Skating Hall of Fame in 1998 and the World Figure Skating Hall of Fame in 1999.

• She is the founder of the Always Dream Foundation, which raises funds and supports children's charities.

• She won the *Dancing with the Stars* competition in 2008.

Taking It Further ★★★★★★★★★★★★★★★★★★★★★★★★★★★★★

Tell children that Yamaguchi lived by her motto, "Always Dream." Discuss why she may have chosen this motto for her life. Then prepare and pass out pages that read, "(Child's name) has a dream to _____." at the top. Have children complete the sentence by writing their own name and a future goal on the lines. Invite them to illustrate their page and then share it with the class. Finally, bind all of the pages together to create a class book titled "Always Dream!"

Book Break ★★★★★★★★★★★★★★★★★★★★★★★★★★★★★★★★★

Kristi Yamaguchi by Elaine A. Kule (Raintree, 2006). This book is filled with pictures and information about Yamaguchi and her fellow skaters.

George

Glue word box 1 here.

by _____

cover

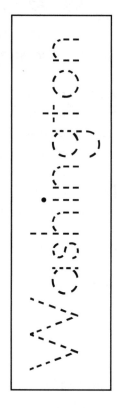

George Washington learned to be a

Glue word box 2 here.

at Mount Vernon.

I

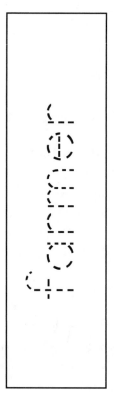

At 21, he became a

Glue word box 3 here.

in the
Virginia army.

2

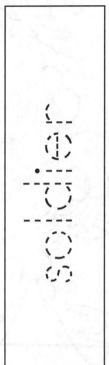

He was a

Glue word box 4 here.

when he led the
American Revolution.

3

booklet backing

Staple pages here.

George Washington was the first

Glue word box 5 here.

of the United States.

4

word box 5

1

Johnny Appleseed's
real name was
John Chapman.

3

Draw 3 🌳s.

He planted them for settlers.

cover

Johnny
Appleseed

by _____

2

Draw 1 🌳.

He loved apple trees.

Draw 8 🌳s.

4

The settlers loved the trees.

Draw 10 🌳s.

5

Johnny planted trees for 50 years.

Draw 1 🍎.

Staple pages here.

6

Thanks for apple trees, Johnny!

booklet backing

Sacagawea traveled west with Lewis and Clark

Sacagawea

by _____

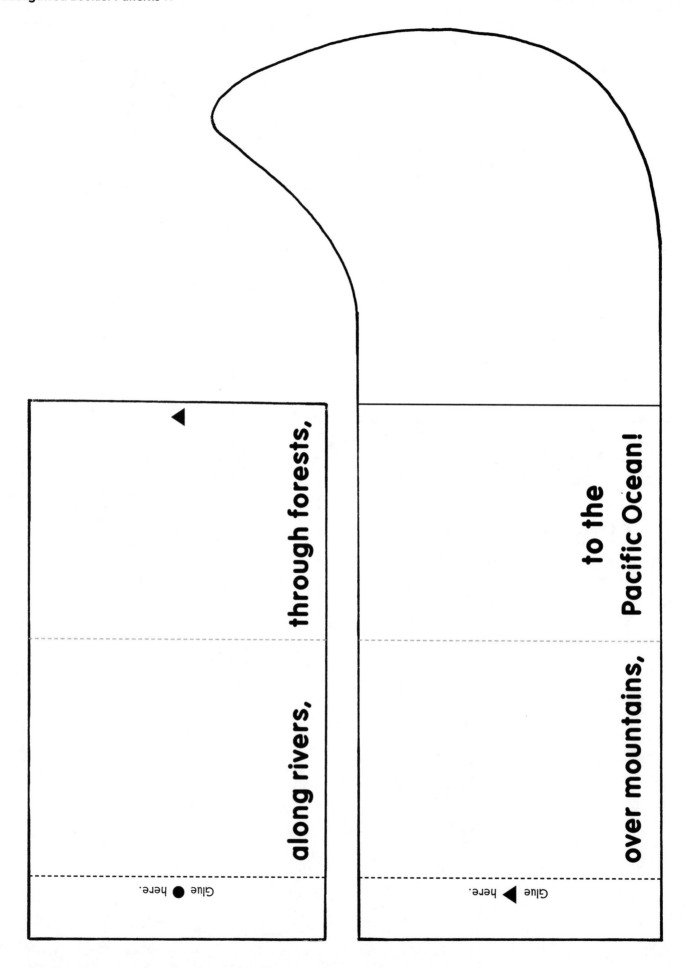

through forests,

along rivers,

Glue ● here.

to the
Pacific Ocean!

over mountains,

Glue ◀ here.

Glue cover here.

cover

Abraham Lincoln

by _____

text strips

Pull tab up.

↑

Abraham
Lincoln
was the

Glue word box here.

president. 1

He was
a very

Glue word box here.

man. 2

Glue ■ here.

He wore
a tall

Glue word box here.

3

He
wrote

Glue word box here.

4

Glue ● here.

He put
the notes

Glue word box here.

his hat! 5

Note:

6

Insert this end through slits.

word boxes

16th	tall	hat.	notes.	in

booklet backing

Susan B. Anthony

SO ALL MAY
VOTE

by _____

Staple pages here.

She helped pass a law that gave American women the right to

_____

- -

_____ .

5

Many years ago, American women could not

_____

- - - - - - - - - - - - - - - - -

_____ .

1

Susan B. Anthony said that women had a right to

_____

- - - - - - - - - - - - - - - - -

_____ .

2

She wrote books about the right to

_____

- - - - - - - - - - - - - - - - -

_____ .

3

She gave speeches about the right to

_____

- - - - - - - - - - - - - - - - -

_____ .

4

Harriet Tubman

by _____

cover

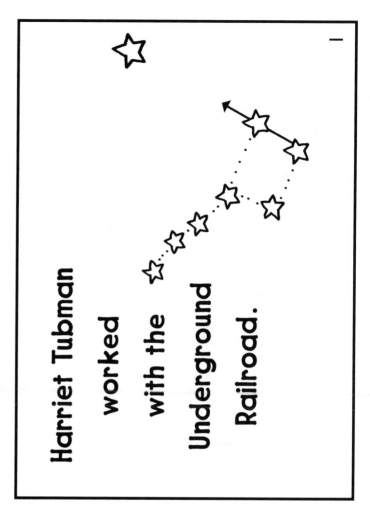

Harriet Tubman worked with the Underground Railroad.

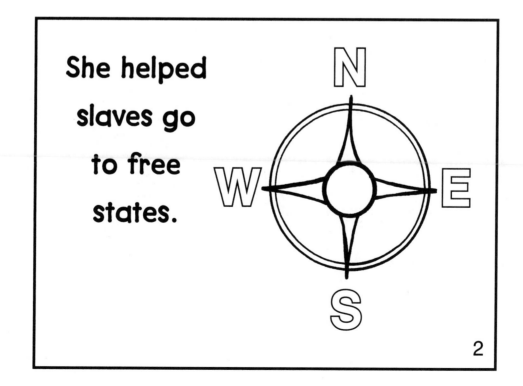

She helped slaves go to free states.

2

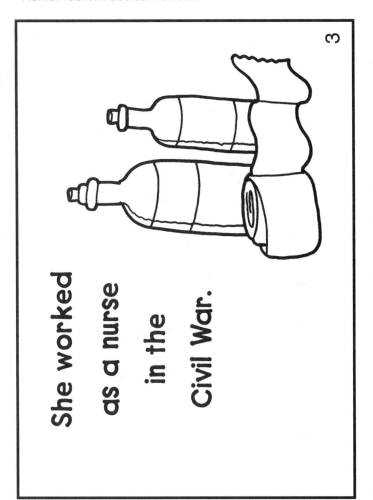

She worked
as a nurse
in the
Civil War.

3

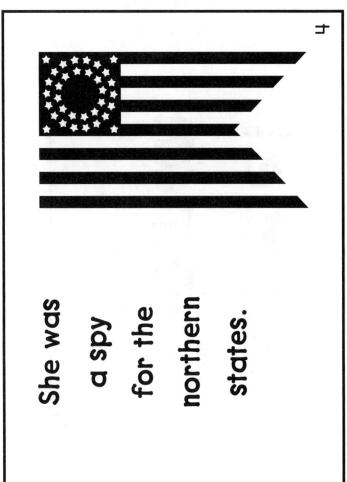

She was
a spy
for the
northern
states.

4

She built
a home for
African
Americans
in need.

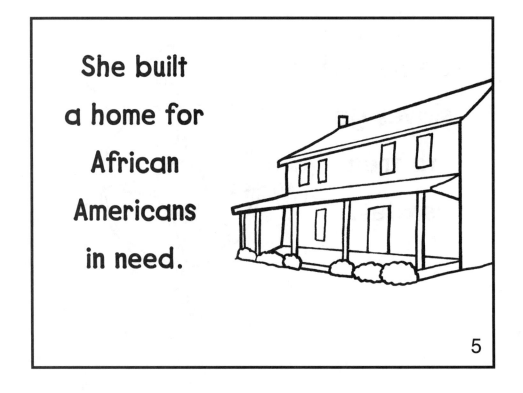

5

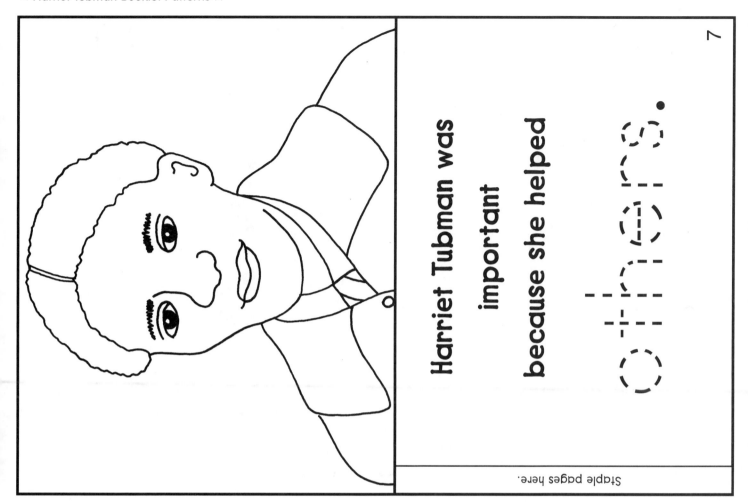

7

Harriet Tubman was important because she helped

others.

Staple pages here.

booklet backing

She worked to get women the right to vote.

VOTES for WOMEN

6

4

She started the American Red Cross.

Staple pages here.

Clara Barton

and

by _____

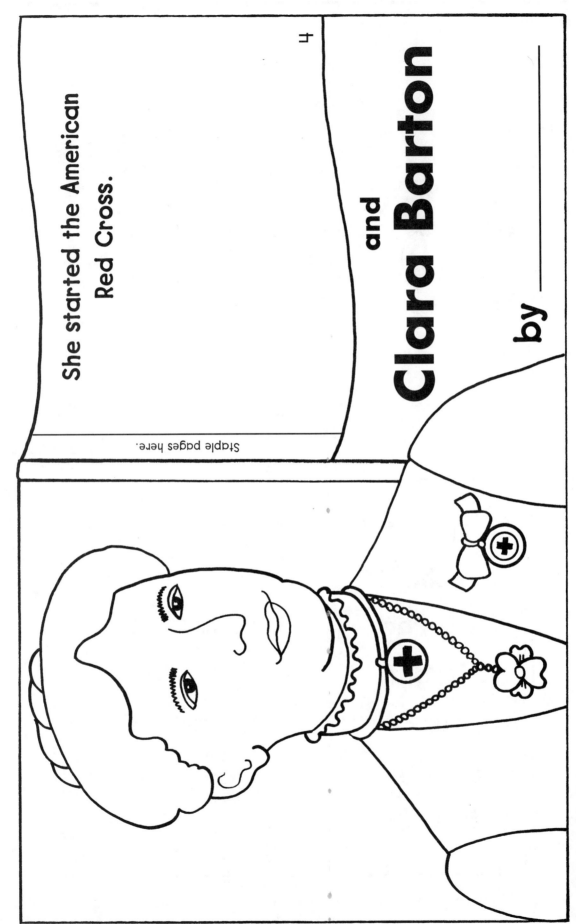

booklet backing

1

Clara Barton wrote letters. She asked people to help Civil War soldiers.

3

She rode a wagon onto the battlefield to help soldiers.

cover

The

American Red Cross

2

She took care of hurt soldiers in her home.

animals,

2

John Muir
wanted to protect
rivers,

1

John Muir:
Conservationist

by _____

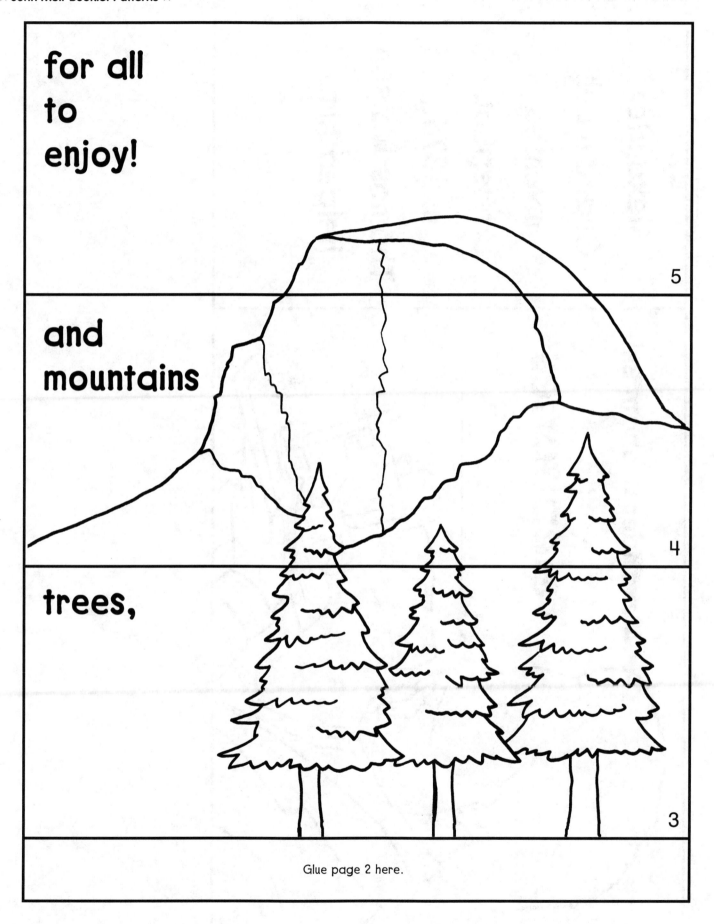

for all
to
enjoy!

5

and
mountains

4

trees,

3

Glue page 2 here.

1

Alexander Graham Bell invented a telephone in 1876. Thomas Watson helped him.

Alexander Graham Bell and

Telephones

by _____

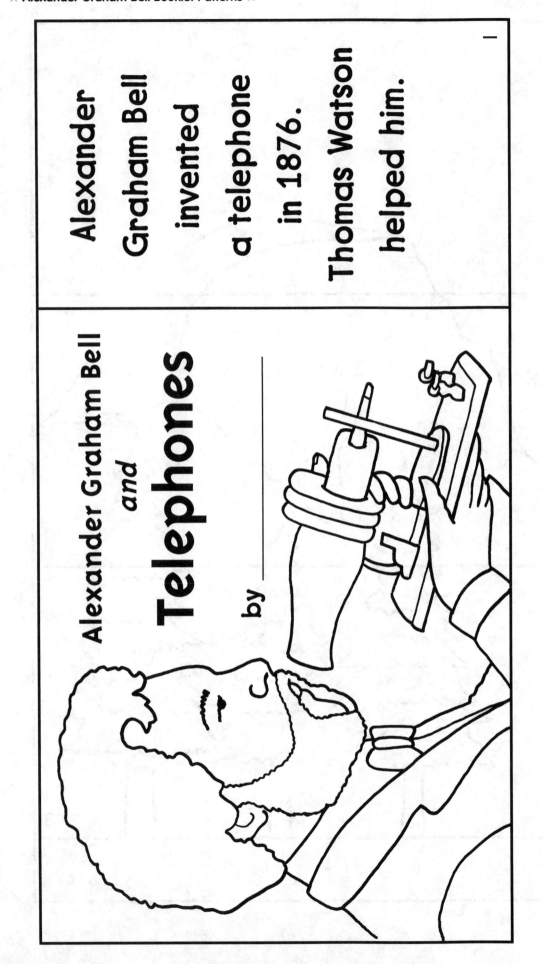

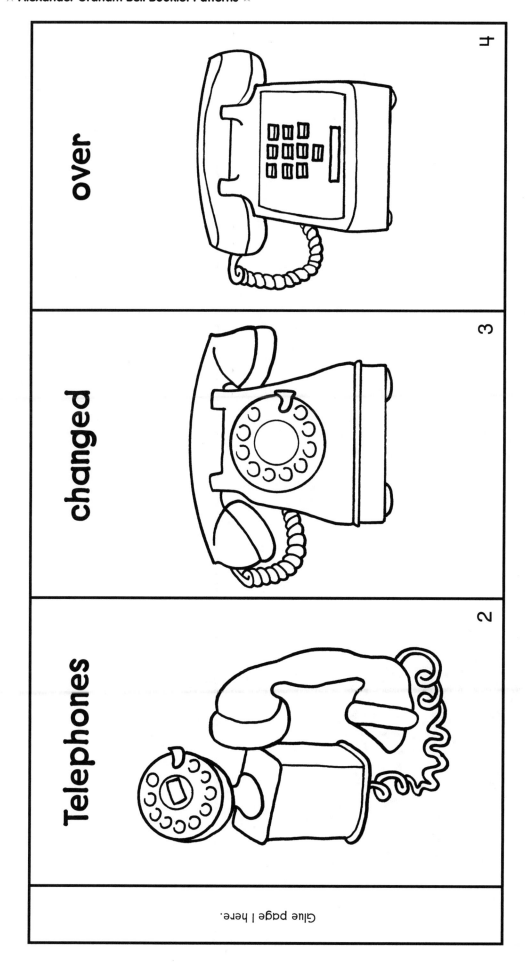

over

4

changed

3

Telephones

2

Glue page I here.

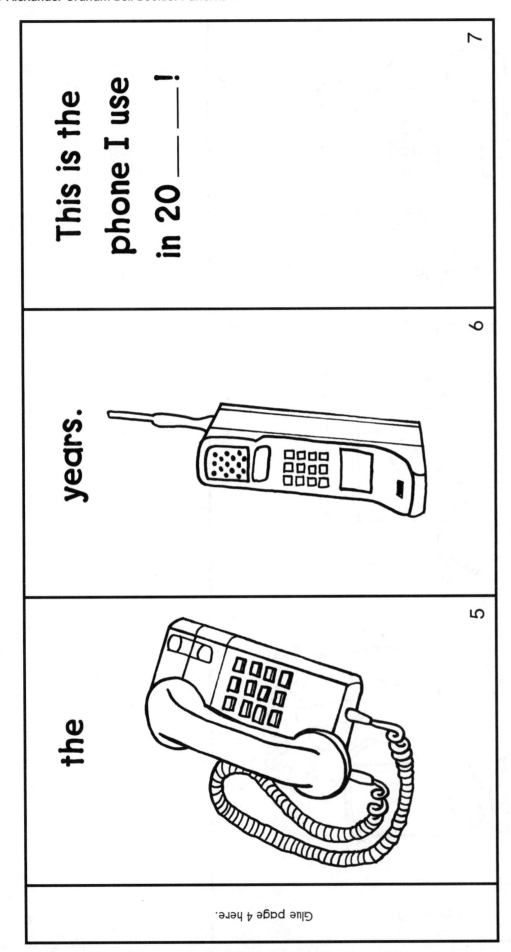

7

This is the phone I use in 20 ___ !

6

years.

5

the

Glue page 4 here.

George Washington
Carver:

Staple pages here.

Glue picture
box here.

He taught them
to grow peanuts!

6

An
Amazing
Scientist

by _____

George Washington Carver

was a scientist

and teacher

at Tuskegee Institute

in Alabama.

—

3

Glue picture box here.

He had them grow crops that helped the soil.

5

Glue picture box here.

He taught them to grow soy beans.

2

Glue picture box here.

Most farmers there only grew cotton.

4

Glue picture box here.

He taught farmers to grow sweet potatoes.

picture boxes

booklet backing

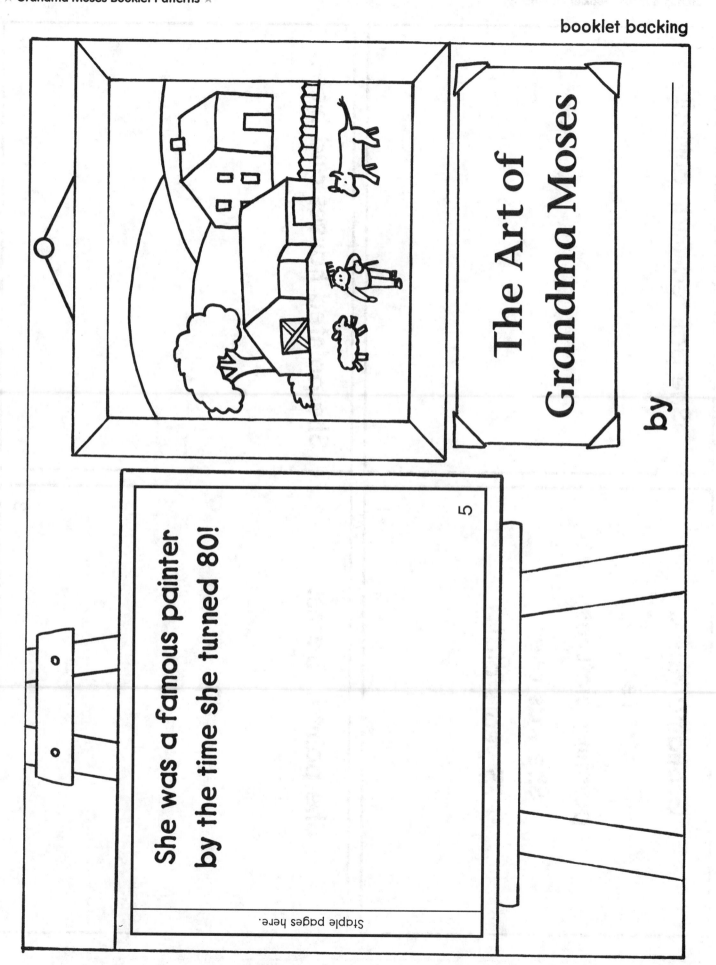

The Art of Grandma Moses

by _____

She was a famous painter by the time she turned 80!

5

Staple pages here.

She painted farm animals.

2

She painted houses and trees.

4

Grandma Moses started painting pictures. She was over 75 years old!

1

She painted barns.

3

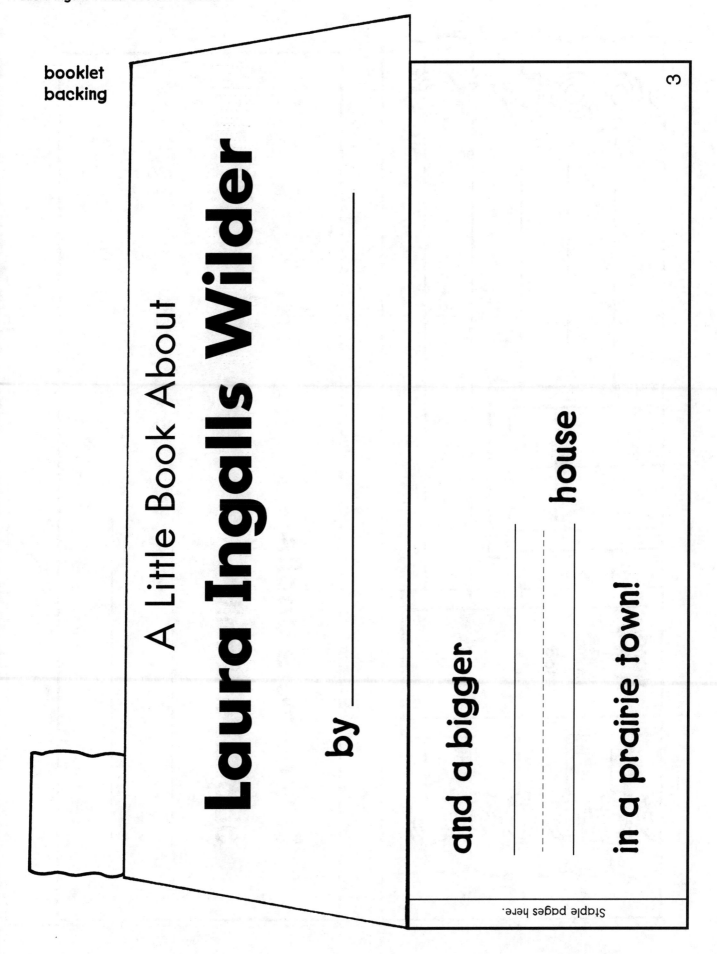

booklet
backing

A Little Book About

Laura Ingalls Wilder

by _____

3

and a bigger _____

_____ house

in a prairie town!

Staple pages here.

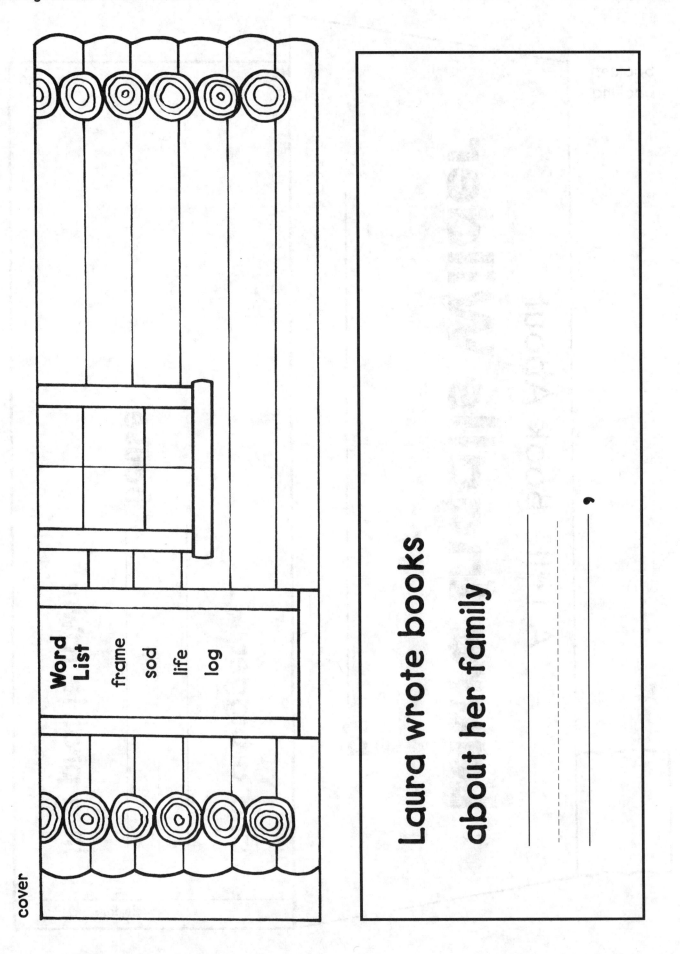

Word List

frame

sod

life

log

cover

Laura wrote books
about her family

a little

_____

house

- - - - -

_____

in the woods,

2

a little

_____

house

- - - - -

_____

on the prairie,

3

booklet backing

Staple pages here.

Then Helen Keller
helped
other blind and deaf

Glue word box 6 here.

6

cover

Helen Keller

by _____

Helen Keller could not
see.
She was

Glue word box 1 here.

.

1

She could not
hear.
She was

Glue word box 2 here.

.

2

---

word box 1

blind

word box 2

deaf

word box 3

communicate

She could not
speak.
It was hard to

Glue word box 3 here.

3

word box 4

teacher

Helen learned from
Anne Sullivan.
Anne was a good

Glue word box 4 here.

4

word box 5

college

Helen loved to
learn.
She graduated from

Glue word box 5 here.

5

word box 6

people

Jim Thorpe:

He won two gold medals!

Staple pages here.

booklet backing

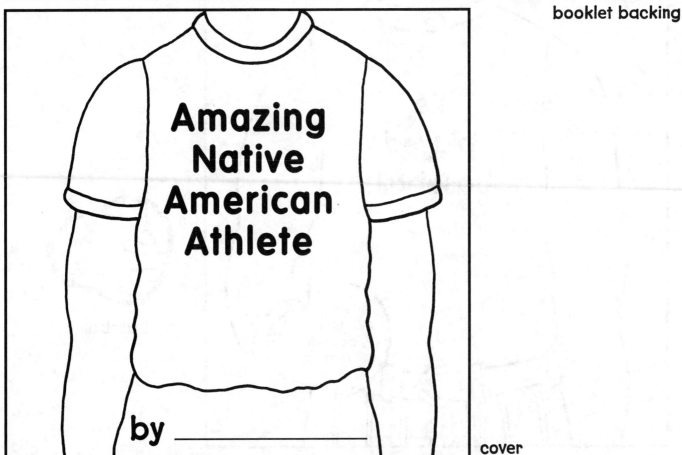

Amazing
Native
American
Athlete

by _____

cover

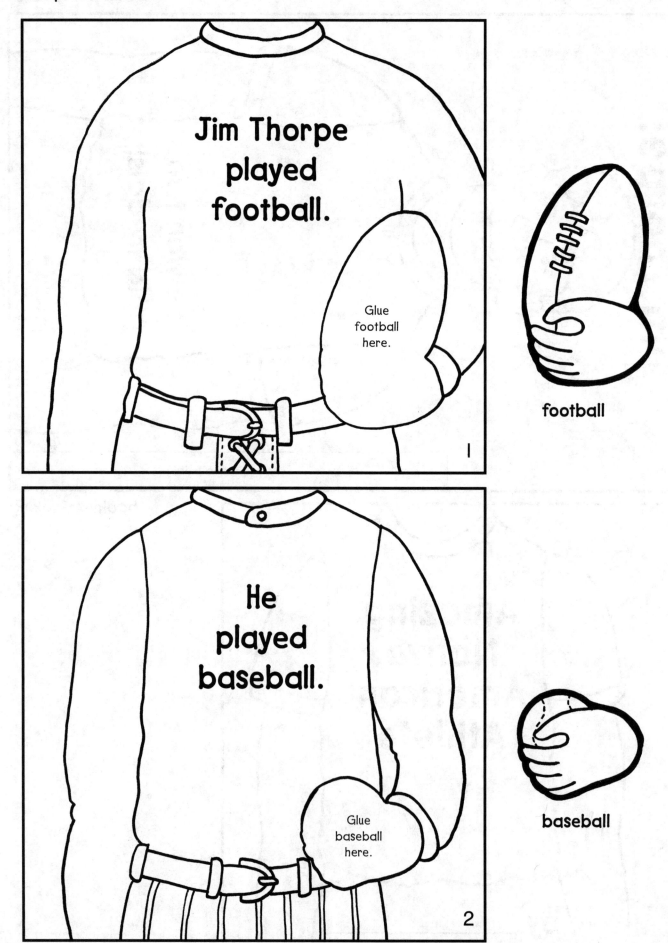

Jim Thorpe played football.

Glue football here.

football

1

He played baseball.

Glue baseball here.

baseball

2

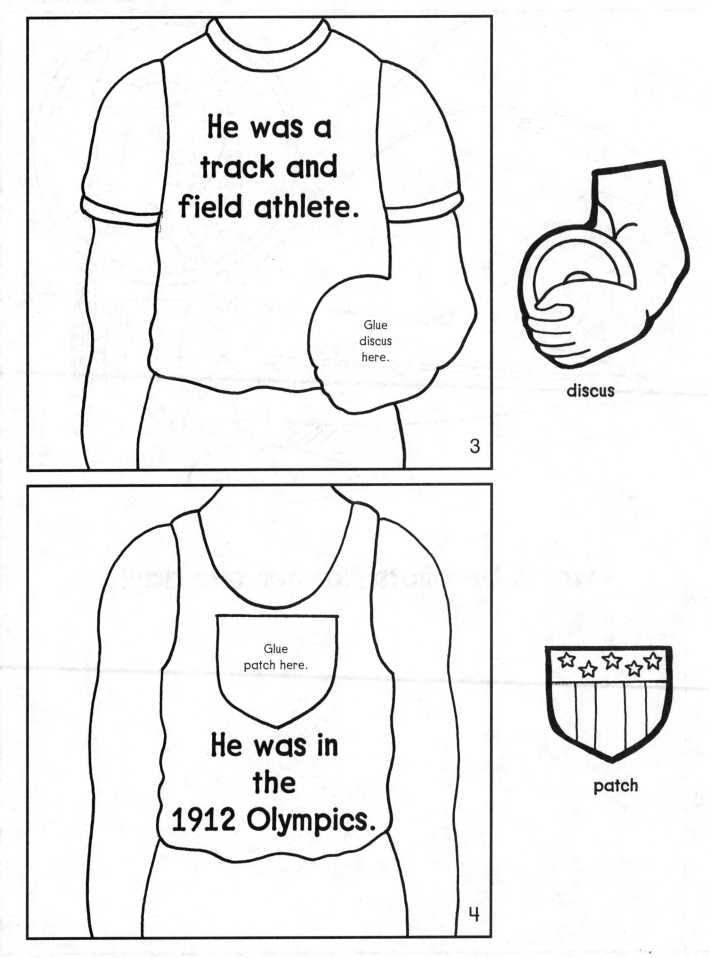

He was a
track and
field athlete.

Glue
discus
here.

3

discus

Glue
patch here.

He was in
the
1912 Olympics.

4

patch

would be pilots like her one day!

Staple pages here.

4

Amelia Earhart:
Record-Breaking Pilot

by _____

cover

Amelia flew across the Atlantic ocean.

I

She flew across the USA.

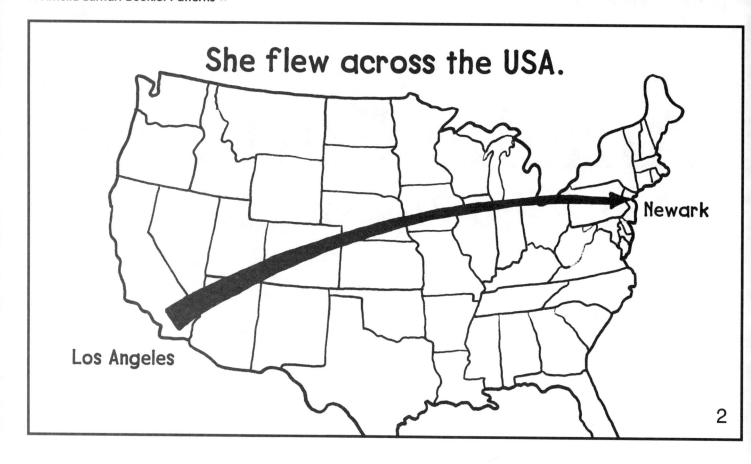

Newark

Los Angeles

2

She hoped that lots of women

3

a
strange
cat,

2

He wrote
about
green
eggs,

1

Guess the Writer

by _____

Dr.
Seuss!

5

What is
this
writer's
name?

4

and
some
Whos.

3

Glue page 2 here.

1

Rachel Carson wrote

Glue word box here.

3

She wrote about

Glue word box here.

cover

Rachel Carson: Science Writer

by _____

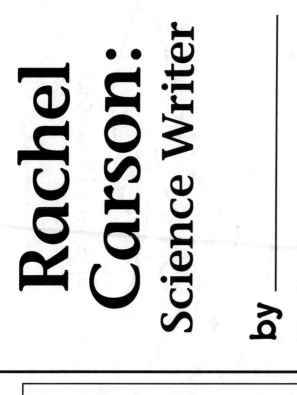

2

She wrote about

Glue word box here.

books.

plants.

animals.

word boxes

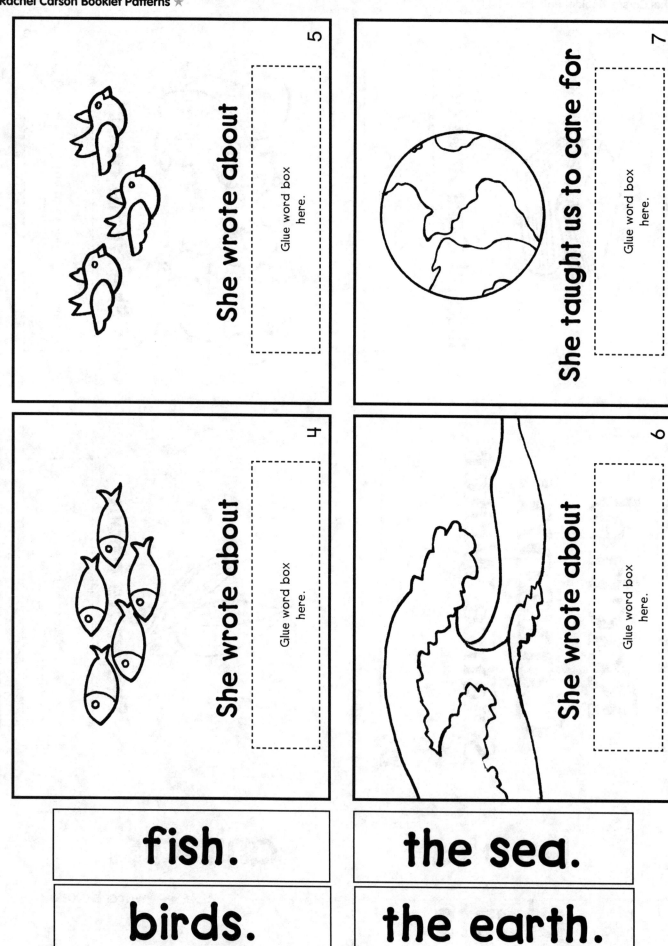

5

She wrote about

Glue word box here.

7

She taught us to care for

Glue word box here.

4

She wrote about

Glue word box here.

6

She wrote about

Glue word box here.

fish.

birds.

the sea.

the earth.

word boxes

Staple pages here.

I would write about

8

"Those who dwell among the beauties and mysteries of the earth are never alone or weary of life."

Glue flap 1 here.

She was a brave African-American woman.

1

Glue flap 3 here.

She did not give up her seat on a bus.

3

Rosa Parks

by _____

cover

Glue flap 2 here.

She lived in Montgomery, Alabama.

2

Glue flap 4 here.

Laws were passed to give all people equal rights.

5

Staple pages here.

booklet backing

WHO was Rosa Parks? 1	WHAT did she do? 3
WHERE did she live? 2	HOW did her actions help others? 4

flaps

Player

Jackie Robinson was the first African American to play Major League baseball.

Jackie Robinson

Baseball Legend

by _____

3

Position

Jackie played first base his rookie year. After that he played second base.

2

Team

Jackie played for the Brooklyn Dodgers.

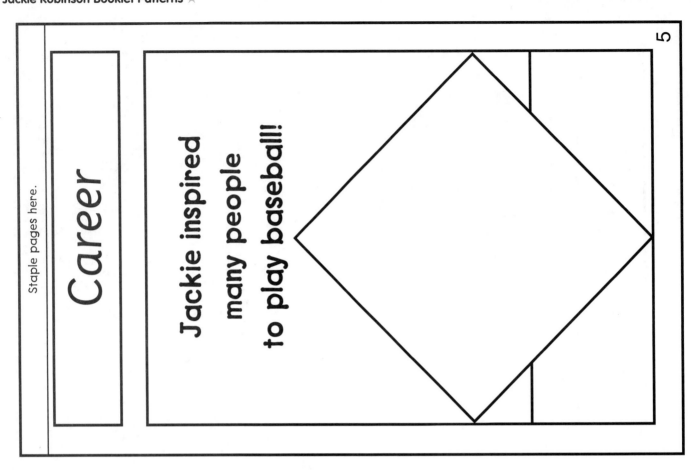

Staple pages here.

Career

Jackie inspired many people to play baseball!

5

Home Runs

He scored more than 100 home runs in six seasons.

4

Cesar Chavez: A Man Who **Cared**

by _____

Cesar Chavez cared about **farm workers.**

7

Staple pages here.

2

Draw farm workers.

4

Draw money.

1

Cesar Chavez helped

Glue word box 1 here.

workers.

3

He helped them get fair

Glue word box 2 here.

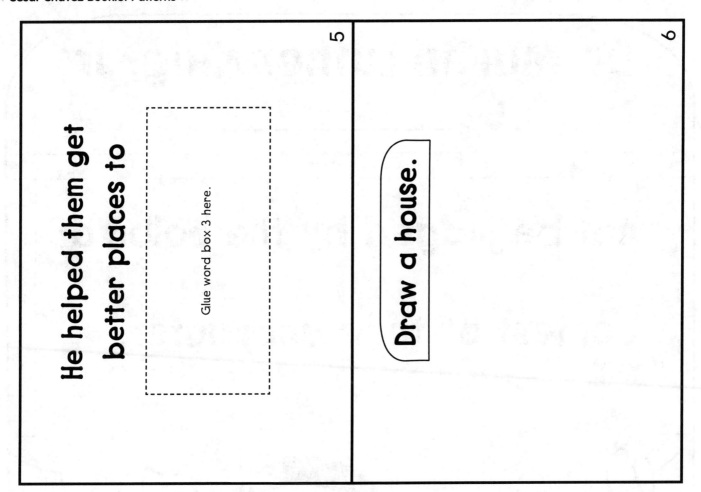

5

He helped them get better places to

Glue word box 3 here.

6

Draw a house.

farm

word box 1

pay.

word box 2

live.

word box 3

Dr. Martin Luther King, Jr.

by _____

Glue top flap here.

Glue left flap here.

Glue right flap here.

not be judged by the color of

content of their character.

Literacy-Building Booklets: Famous Americans © 2010 by Lucia Kemp Henry, Scholastic Teaching Resources

top flap

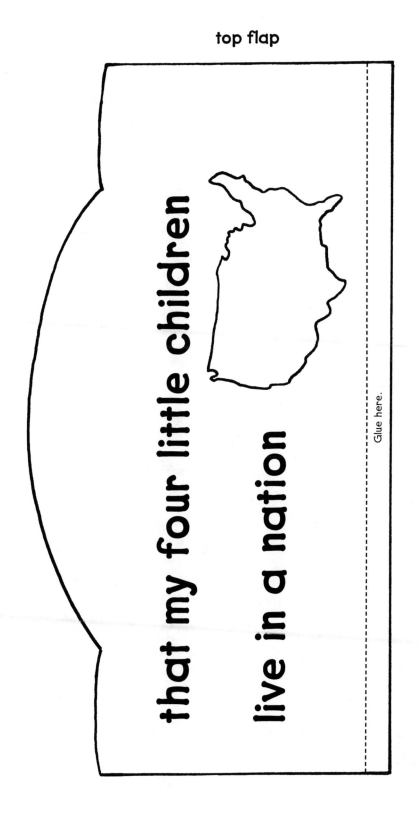

that my four little children

live in a nation

Glue here.

right flap

left flap

Glue here.

Glue here.

their skin

I have a dream

will one day

where they will

but by the

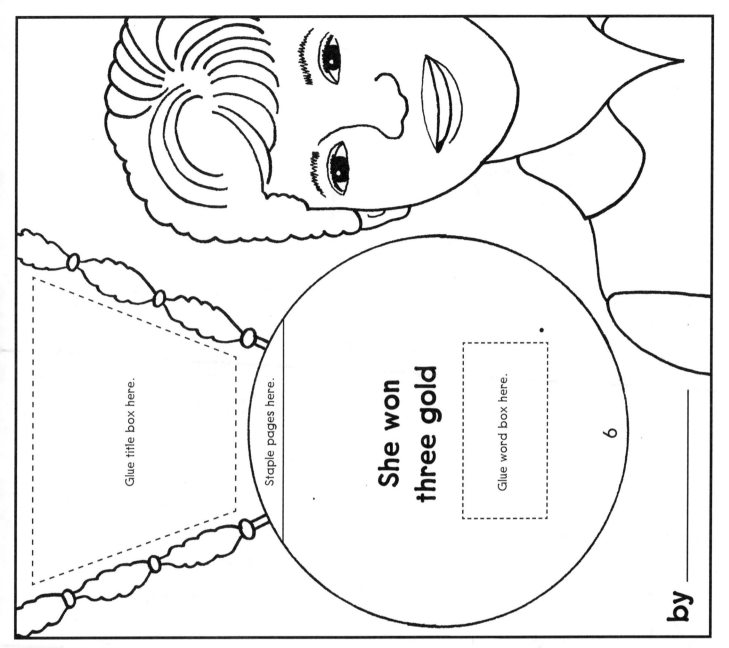

booklet backing

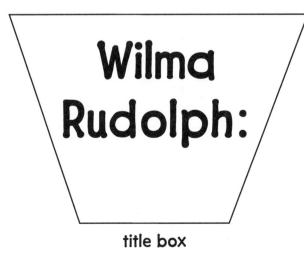

Wilma Rudolph:

title box

child	strong
ran	Olympics
races	medals

word boxes

cover

Sprinting Star

by

_____

When
Wilma was a

Glue word box here.

,

she wore
leg braces.

1

She
worked hard to
make her legs

Glue word box here.

.

2

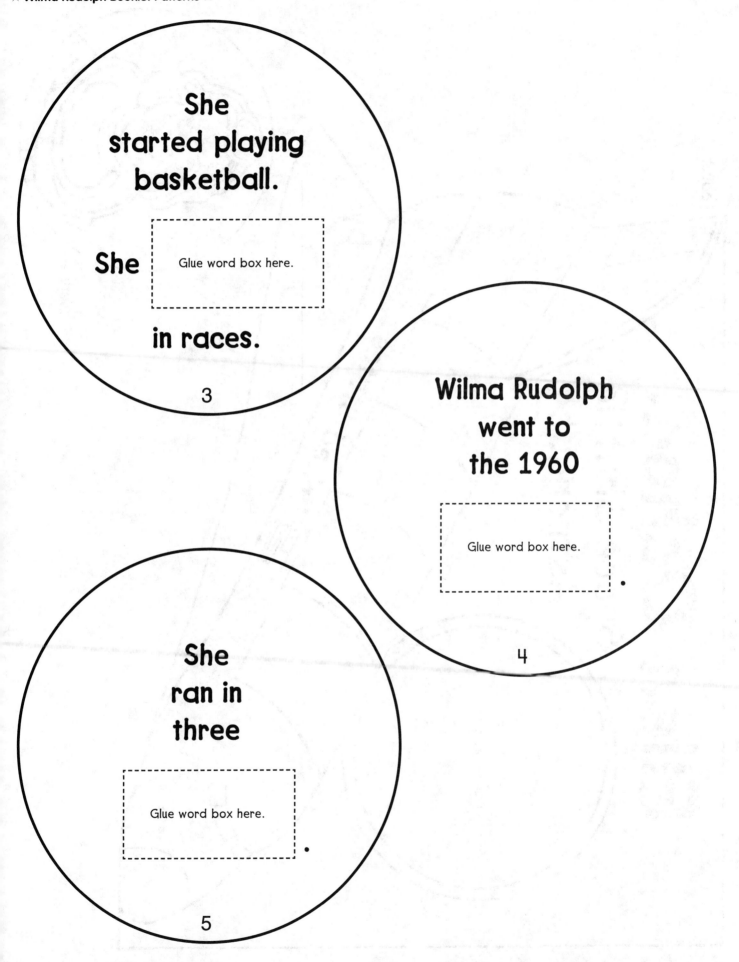

She
started playing
basketball.

She [Glue word box here.]

in races.

3

Wilma Rudolph
went to
the 1960

[Glue word box here.] .

4

She
ran in
three

[Glue word box here.] .

5

cover

Ellen Ochoa:
Space Shuttle Astronaut

Glue picture here.

by

United States

picture

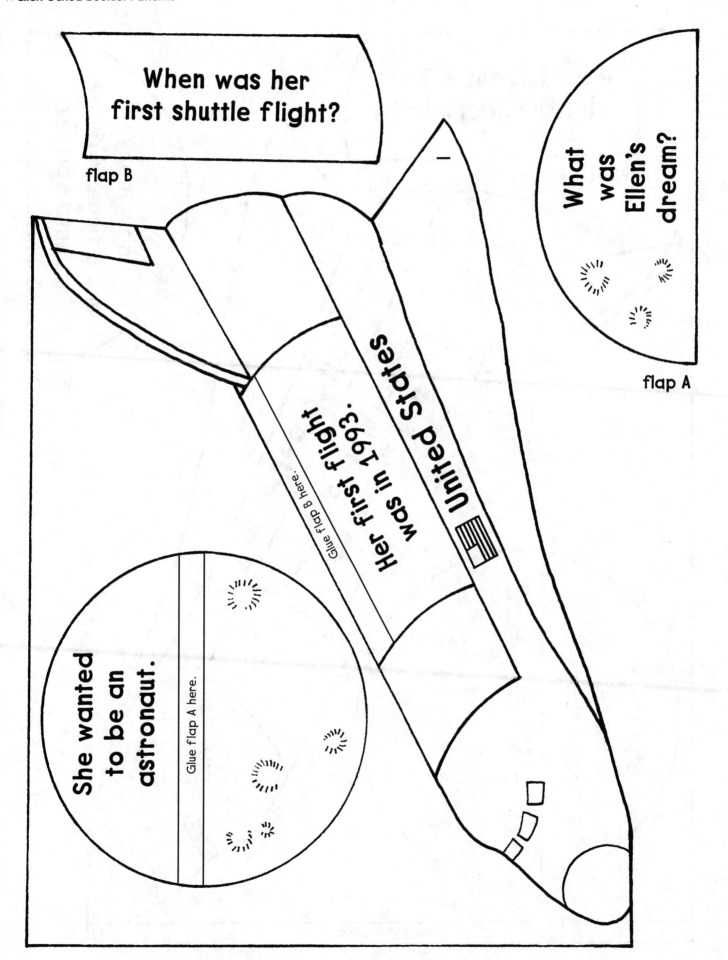

When was her
first shuttle flight?

flap B

What was Ellen's dream?

flap A

Glue flap B here.

Her first flight was in 1993.

United States

She wanted to be an astronaut.

Glue flap A here.

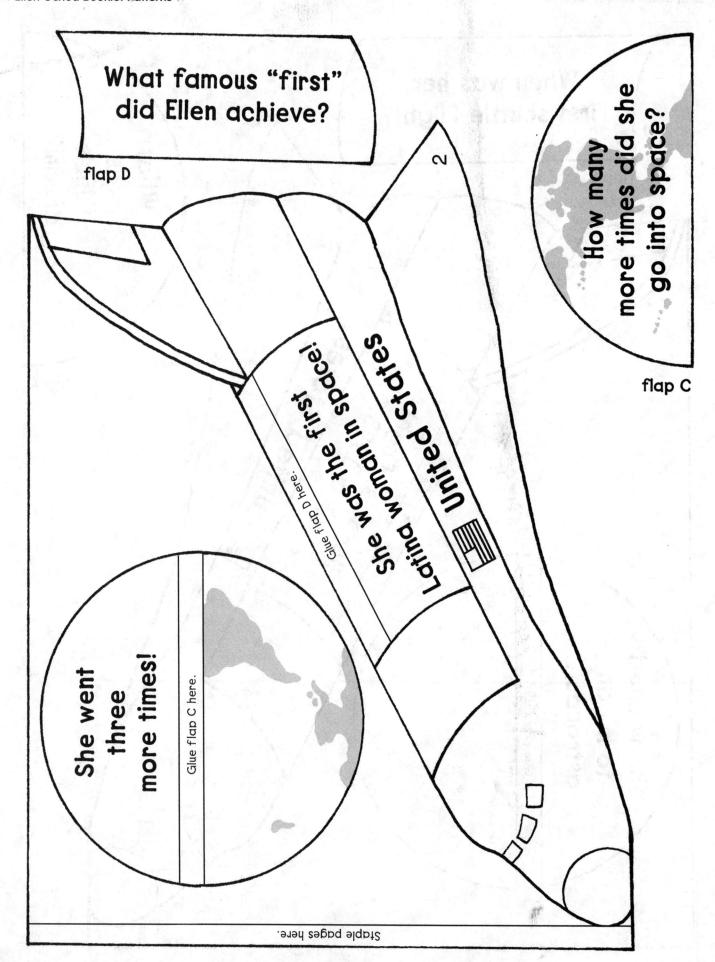

What famous "first"
did Ellen achieve?

flap D

2

How many
more times did she
go into space?

flap C

Glue flap D here.

She was the first!

She woman in space!

Latina

United States

She went
three
more times!

Glue flap C here.

Staple pages here.

5

Barack Obama— our 44th

president.

Glue flag here.

Staple pages here.

booklet backing

Barack Obama

44th President of the United States

cover

by _____

Glue Capitol here.

Barack Obama was a United States Senator.

1

Glue logo here.

He decided to run for President of the United States.

2

Glue seal here.

He was elected to be our president in 2008.

3

 Literacy-Building Booklets: Famous Americans © 2010 by Lucia Kemp Henry, Scholastic Teaching Resources

Glue White House here.

Barack Obama
moved into
the White House
with his family.

4

Capitol

logo

seal

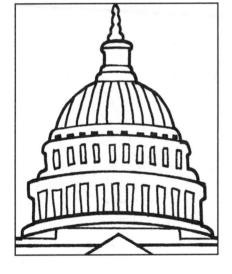

White House

flag

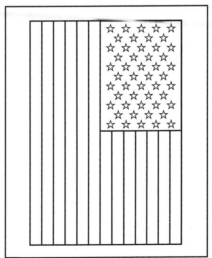

Kristi Yamaguchi

by _____

Staple pages here.

That same year, she also won an Olympic gold medal!

3 ●

2 ●

4 ●

●

1992

5

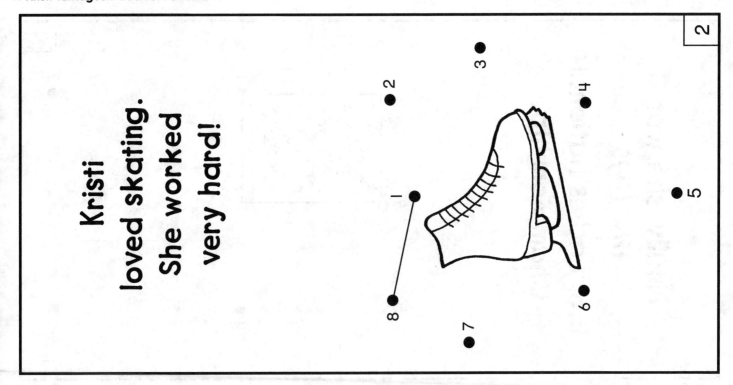

Kristi
loved skating.
She worked
very hard!

2

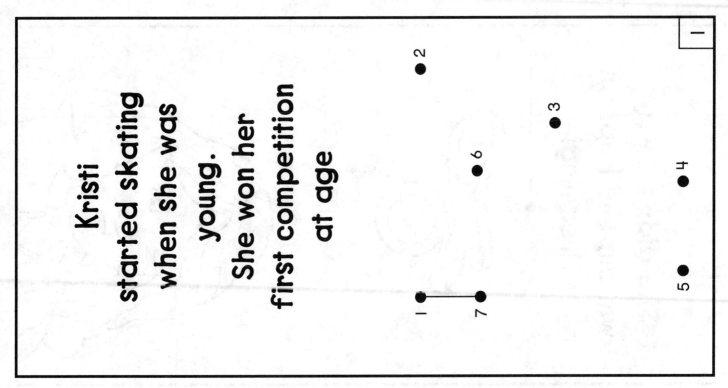

Kristi
started skating
when she was
young.
She won her
first competition
at age

1

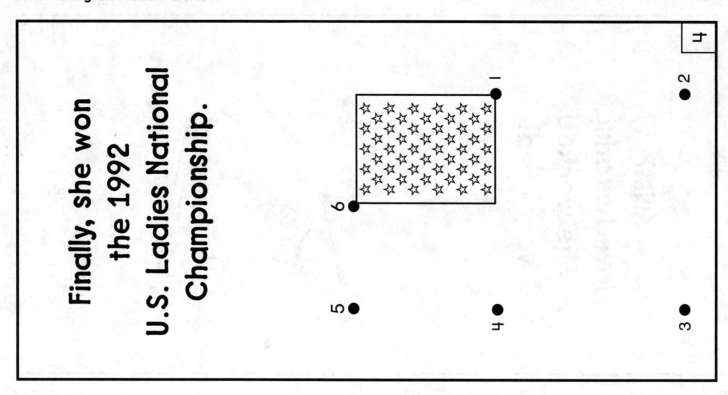

Finally, she won the 1992 U.S. Ladies National Championship.

4

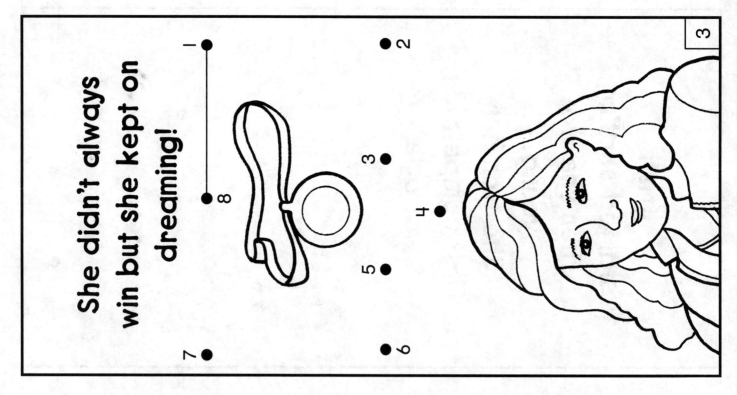

She didn't always win but she kept on dreaming!

3